Swim, Bike, Run

Glenn Town, PhD
Wheaton College, Wheaton, IL

Todd Kearney, MS
Splash, Mash, Dash, Lindenhurst, IL

Human Kinetics Publishers

Library of Congress Cataloging-in-Publication Data

Town, Glenn P., 1949-
    Swim, bike, run / Glenn Town, Todd Kearney.
        p.   cm.
    Includes bibliographical references (p.) and index.
    ISBN 0-87322-513-9
    1. Triathlon--Training.   I. Kearney, Todd, 1960-   . II. Title.
    GV1060.73.T68   1994
    796.4'07--dc20   93-24695
                                                                                 CIP

ISBN: 0-87322-513-9

Acquisitions Editor: Brian Holding; **Developmental Editor:** Mary Fowler; **Assistant Editors:** Sally Bayless, Dawn Roselund; **Copyeditor:** Barbara Walsh; **Proofreaders:** Anne Meyer Byler, Pam Johnson; **Indexer:** Theresa J. Schaefer; **Production Director:** Ernie Noa; **Typesetter:** Yvonne Winsor; **Text Designer:** Keith Blomberg; **Layout Artist:** Tara Welsch; **Cover Designer:** Jack Davis; **Photographer (cover):** F-Stock; **Interior Art:** Tim Offenstein, Gretchen Walters; **Printer:** United Graphics

Human Kinetics books are available at special discounts for bulk purchase. Special editions or book excerpts can also be created to specification. For details, contact the Special Sales Manager at Human Kinetics.

Printed in the United States of America   10   9   8   7   6   5   4   3   2

Human Kinetics
P.O. Box 5076, Champaign, IL 61825-5076
1-800-747-4457

Canada: Human Kinetics, Box 24040, Windsor, ON N8Y 4Y9
1-800-465-7301 (in Canada only)

Europe: Human Kinetics, P.O. Box IW14, Leeds LS16 6TR, England
0532-781708

Australia: Human Kinetics, P.O. Box 80, Kingswood 5062, South Australia
618-374-0433

New Zealand: Human Kinetics, P.O. Box 105-231, Auckland 1
(09) 309-2259

To the one and only God, who has provided more than just the physical strength to successfully finish a difficult race.

Contents

Part IV—Competing and More 185

Foreword

Two schools of thought make up the education process. One side promotes the theoretical, or "book learning," approach. The other advocates practical, or "hands on," instruction. As a triathlete, you can't lean to one side or another. You need both.

Consider the sport. Triathlons began as an experiment in the mid-1970s; an extension of a group's running workout set the wheels in motion for an entirely new sport. But was it really new, or just three existing disciplines lumped together to form a unique hybrid event? And how did you train for this beast? In theory, you simply could train like any self-respecting swimmer, cyclist, or runner, all at the same time. And this is what we did for a while in the late '70s. But after a while, it became obvious that this approach was not possible at any high level for any length of time. There was a definite point of diminishing returns when your log book showed 500 miles cycling and 80 miles running for one week.

Enter the "experts." When it was obvious that triathlon wasn't going away, a number of exercise physiologists started to look at this new event and theorize how one might go about training properly for it. Some of the ideas made sense, while others were not in line with what I and other top athletes had found to be successful training programs.

It seems now, in the early '90s, that the hard and fast rules of athletic training developed in the labs are beginning to merge with the growing experience and knowledge of competitors who have learned by years of trial and error.

Swim, Bike, Run is an opportunity for triathletes of all levels to access a solid base of information that is equal parts science, experience, and field-tested triathlon theory. It will provide a helpful guide to newcomers and an excellent vehicle for experienced triathletes to refresh their knowledge of the basics. Glenn Town and Todd Kearney have taken their knowledge from the lab and combined it with their hands-on experience of triathlon competition to produce an excellent learning source. I think you'll find it helpful in avoiding many of the pitfalls I made years ago, before this type of book was available.

Scott Tinley

Preface

Welcome to the world of triathlon training! Whether you are new to this three-in-one event or a veteran performer, you've made a good decision to increase your knowledge of triathlon training and competition. Your success in triathlons is only as great as the time you invest. By taking a systematic and scientific approach to your training, you can get the edge on the competition. *Swim, Bike, Run* helps you do just that, giving special tips to make you a better swimmer, cyclist, and runner.

Swim, Bike, Run shows you how to meet your athletic goals—whether you're a beginner working toward your first triathlon or an old hand training for local, national, or international competition. The book provides practical advice stemming from our laboratory research, our personal study and experience, and the lessons we've learned from coaching triathletes. We've broken down the scientific principles of physiology, biomechanics, nutrition, and psychology and developed an easy-to-understand approach that will guide you in establishing your training goals and designing or improving your unique training program. Take advantage of our proven methods for planning, implementing, and monitoring your training, and you can design a program that's perfect for your needs.

Swim, Bike, Run covers it all, including counting the costs, getting and fitting the necessary clothing and equipment, maintaining your bicycle, learning and perfecting proper technique, preventing injury, and preparing yourself during race week and on race day. Competition places different demands on triathletes than on single-sport endurance athletes. We offer excellent technique instruction aimed at letting you get the most out of your training for each of the three sports. More importantly, we show you how to sequence your training so that you perform your best from start to finish come race day.

If you're a veteran triathlete, you know the importance of good nutrition and positive thinking. Endurance athletes who neglect their diet and mental approach pay the price in terms of injury, illness, and poor performance. *Swim, Bike, Run* will help you avoid these pitfalls with sound nutritional advice and proper mental training.

The triathlon is one of the most grueling and challenging events in sport. The training and competition tests the physical and mental limits of all those who participate. If you haven't already, we hope you accept the triathlon challenge, for it has enduring rewards. If you already are a seasoned competitor, learn what it takes to be the best triathlete you can be. Our purpose in writing this book is to help you *Swim, Bike, Run* better than ever.

Acknowledgment

Thanks to Scott Naylor, Everett Schleter, Jim Horn, Bill Ornt, and Wanda Kearney for critiquing the chapters. Thanks to Bill Favata for doing much of the photographic work. Thanks to Cannondale, Aerospoke, Tinley Performance Wear, Oakley, and O'Neill for providing much of the equipment used in this book. Appreciation also is extended to the staff of Human Kinetics Publishers.

Credits

Tables 2.1, 2.2, and 2.3 are from *Science of Cycling* (pp. 125, 134, 69) by E.R. Burke, 1986, Champaign, IL: Human Kinetics. Copyright 1986 by Edmund Burke. Reprinted by permission.

Table 2.5 is courtesy of Nytro Multisport, Enanitas, CA, 1-800-697-8007.

Figure 3.1 is from *Swimming* (p. 14) by D.L. Costill, E.W. Maglischo, and A.B. Richardson, 1992, Oxford: Blackwell Scientific Publications. Copyright 1992 by Blackwell Scientific Publications. Reprinted and adapted with the compliments of Blackwell Scientific Publications Ltd.

Figure 3.5 is from *Swimming Faster* (p. 67) by E. Maglischo, 1982, Palo Alto: Mayfield Publishing Company. Copyright 1982 by Mayfield Publishing Company. Adapted by permission.

Figure 4.1 is from E.F. Coyle, M.E. Feltner, S.A. Kautz, M.T. Hamilton, S.J. Montain, A.M. Baylor, I.D. Abraham, and G.W. Petrek, "Physiological and Biomechanical Factors Associated With Elite Endurance Cycling Performance," *Medicine and Science in Sport and Exercise*, 23(1), p. 101, 1991. Copyright © 1991 by the American College of Sports Medicine. Reprinted by permission.

Figure 4.2 is from *The Physiology and Biomechanics of Cycling* (p. 91) by I. Faria and P. Cavanagh, 1978, New York: John Wiley & Sons, Inc. Reprinted by permission of Peter R. Cavanagh.

Figure 4.3 is from *Science of Cycling* (p. 155) by E.R. Burke, 1986, Champaign, IL: Human Kinetics. Copyright 1986 by Edmund Burke. Reprinted by permission.

Figures 2.13 and 4.4 and Table 8.3 are from *Science of Triathlon Training and Competition* (pp. 77, 69, 28) by G.P. Town, 1985, Champaign, IL: Human Kinetics. Copyright 1985 by Glenn P. Town. Reprinted by permission.

Figure 4.5 is from "The Aerodynamics of Human-Powered Land Vehicles," A.C. Gross, C.R. Kyle, D.J. Malewicki, *Scientific American*, December, 1983, p. 145. Copyright © 1983 by Scientific American, Inc. All Rights Reserved.

Figure 6.1 is from *Serious Training for Serious Athletes* (p. 37) by R.H. Sleamaker, 1989, Champaign, IL: Leisure Press. Copyright 1989 by Robert Hayes Sleamaker. Reprinted by permission.

Table 6.1 is from *Training Distance Runners* (p. 157) by D.E. Martin and P.N. Coe, 1991, Champaign, IL: Human Kinetics. Copyright 1991 by David E. Martin and Peter N. Coe. Reprinted by permission.

Special Thanks To

Part I

Getting Started

The exciting world of triathlons—swimming, biking, and running—is advancing into the forefront of endurance sports. If you are thinking about getting involved, you no doubt have lots of questions and there is indeed much information to know to participate in a triathlon. If you're an experienced triathlete, keeping up with the constant changes in gear, utilizing the most productive training methods, keeping track of the number and types of events, and striking a balance between your private life and life as a triathlete can be overwhelming. We can help you achieve your goals.

In this part we will introduce you to the types of multisport races that are available and discuss the demands placed on multisport athletes. You will get help in deciding how you can fit all there is to know and do into your current lifestyle.

You will find out about the equipment and clothing needed to participate in triathlon training and racing. You'll discover state-of-the-art innovations that will help you to improve your training and performance. Given the myriad of items required, we point out the "must haves," warn you about the seemingly optional items, and estimate how much you will need to spend to get involved and develop in this sport.

The bicycle is the most expensive item and the only mechanical apparatus in the triathlon. We'll help you decide on a bicycle and fit yourself to it.

Chapter 1

Becoming a Triathlete

Ever since the first triathlon in the mid-1970s, the number of participants in multisport events has been growing. Racing in any endurance sport is fun, but the triathlon offers a special combination of events—swimming, biking, and running.

You might not think that combining events is strange, but go back to the mid-'70s. The running boom had started, but by no means was everyone a runner. Not many people were involved in bicycle racing, and they had never heard of Greg LeMond. Swimming saw a tremendous increase in interest when Mark Spitz won all his medals in the 1972 Summer Olympics, but it never became a sport that adults turned to in great numbers.

In fact, the first Ironman triathlon in 1978 drew just 15 racers for an entry fee of $5! And as far as rapid growth is concerned, the field of contestants the second year was no bigger than the first. But the uniqueness and difficulty of this event inspired people to go out and train. The turning point in the Ironman's popularity was perhaps when ABC television showed Julie Moss crawling the final 100 meters to the finish line in February 1982. Millions of people were touched by her efforts, and some of those decided to follow in her triathlete footsteps.

The triathlon was billed as the sport of the '80s, and from all accounts the sport has lived up to the prediction. What began as a dare among several endurance athletes has become the challenge of hundreds of thousands of distance competitors. What began as an ultradistance event, attracting only the most daring, has diversified. Those wishing to pursue the challenge of the triathlon can now start short (swim .5 mi, bike 12.4 mi, run 3.1 mi) and progress to the challenge of longer distances such as the Ironman—2.4-mi swim, 112-mi bike ride, 26.2-mi run. Regardless of the distance attempted, there is tremendous satisfaction and personal reward for those who compete with one goal in mind—to finish encouraged!

The boom of interest in the triathlon was quickly followed by unique variations on the multisport theme. Duathlons, formerly biathlons, are now extremely popular; this challenge eliminates the swim event (the most difficult for many athletes) and typically is a run-bike-run race. Other multisport events include canoeing, cross-country skiing, or even snowshoeing. Whatever combination of events you choose, the challenge remains the same—to pursue the outer limits of your physical and mental endurance. This challenge first attracted the masses in the form of the running marathon. For most, the victory was in finishing, and during the '70s, thousands of runners attempted and conquered this endurance test. By the '80s, though, the mystique of the marathon had faded for many athletes, paving the way for a favorable response to the triathlon challenge. And if the 1980s offer us any prediction about the future of multisport endurance events, we can safely assume these events are here to stay.

As with all challenges in sport, successful completion is only as great as the preparation time an athlete invests. The way you prepare for competition should be systematic and scientific; you must pay attention to both the obvious and the not-so-obvious concerns related to your event. Not only do multisport athletes have to master the proper techniques of each event, but they must also discover how to sequence the events properly, enabling them to avoid injury and finish encouraged. Fatigue is cumulative and carries over from one event to another. Proper training for multisport events encompasses much more than training for a single sport.

Consider three things you *do not* need to be a triathlete.

- You do not need the speed and endurance of a professional triathlete; you just have to want to do your best. Let's face it, genetics has a great deal to do with ability, and few of us have "elite athlete" genes. But we all can have an intense desire to finish something we've set our minds on.

- You need not spend the same amount of time training that a pro spends. Training six hours a day might sound like fun (if your job didn't get in the way), but it is much harder mentally and physically than you think. However, you can have fun and even achieve quality performances on considerably less training.

- You do not need to spend your entire life savings. Buying reasonably priced equipment, and buying only what you need, can keep competing in triathlons within reach of most budgets.

A number of considerations should pass through your mind before you sign up for any race. Consider the length of the race you are attempting. How long do you have to train? Think about the demands of multisport athletics. Evaluate your abilities; you always need to be honest with yourself about what you can do. If you are new to multisport competition, you need to know the various distances of most triathlons. The following information will help you decide how to train, how to determine what commitments you must make, and how to select the types of races for which you want to train. Some athletes enjoy the shorter distances more, others the longer distances. Every person is different, and triathlons welcome all participants!

Types of Races

In what distance race do you want to participate? All triathlons are not the same; the ratio between swim, bike, and run distances changes, and the type of endurance athlete who will do well in a given distance varies. The longest races are more than 10 times the distance of the shortest, with a corresponding difference in the times of completion. See Table 1.1 for the common distances triathletes race.

Triathlons

The *sprint* distance triathlon is the shortest competitive race category. Sprint distances range between 0.3 and 1 km (.24–.62 mi) for the swim, 8 and 25 km (5–15.5 mi) for the bike, and 1.5 and 5 km (1–3.1 mi) for the run.

The *international* distance triathlon is composed of a 1- to 2-km (.62–1.2-mi) swim, a 25- to 50-km (15.5–31-mi) bike, and a 5- to 10-km (3.1–6.2-mi) run. Olympic distance races include a 1.5-km (0.93-mi) swim, a 40-km (24.8-mi) bike, and a 10-km (6.2-mi) run. The time required to finish this race is similar to that for a marathon run. Long distance

Table 1.1
Race Distances in Triathlons

Name	Swim distance (mi)	Bike distance (mi)	Run distance (mi)
Sprint	0.5	12.4	3.1
International	0.93	24.8	6.2
Long	1.2	56.0	13.1
Ultra	2.4	112.0	26.2

triathlons such as the Half-Ironman are true tests of endurance and are an important stepping-stone to longer distances such as the Ironman. The distances involved range between 2 and 4 km (1.2–2.0 mi) for the swim, 50 and 100 km (31–62 mi) for the bike, and 10 and 30 km (6.2–19 mi) for the run.

The Ironman distance triathlon is the granddaddy of all triathlons. This grueling test of endurance has been the race that has inspired many triathletes to train. Most people associate the Ironman event with Hawaii, but Ironman distance races are held all over the world. The current Ironman series of races begins in New Zealand in March; subsequently, events take place in Australia, Germany, Japan, Canada, and finally Hawaii in October—six Ironman races in seven months! The pros do not race in every one, but the series winner will likely race in five of them.

In medium and long-range distances such as the Half-Ironman and Ironman, swimming is less important than in the sprint and international distances. If you are a poor swimmer but are not ready for longer distance events, look for races that break down the segments differently than do the four standard distance races. You can use the following ratios to determine the relative length of the segments in a nonstandard-distance triathlon. In sprint or international distance triathlons the bike segment is 26.7 times as long as the swim segment, and the run segment is 6.7 times as long as the swim segment. In the ultra and long distance races the bike segment is 46.7 times as long as the swim segment, and the run segment is 10.9 times as long as swim segment. In the shorter distance races, swimming makes up a greater percentage of the race than it does in the longer distance races. A triathlete whose best skill is swimming benefits from shorter distance races. The percentages taken by biking and running do not differ greatly in any of the four standard-distance races.

Duathlons

The standard-distance duathlon is composed of a 5-km run, a 30-km bike, and another 5-km run and takes about as much time to complete as a half-marathon run. This distance, called the *international short-course duathlon*, is by far the most popular distance. Less popular is the *international long-course duathlon* distance—a 5-km run, a 40-km bike, and a 5-km run.

In recent years, duathletes have begun competing in an ultra-type event of their own. The Powerman in Zofingen, Switzerland, consists of a 7.5-km run, a 150-km bike, and a 30-km run. The bike segment requires steep climbs, and the 30-km run takes place mostly on a mountainous trail through wooded countryside. What a test!

The Demands of Multisport Athletics

Regardless of the distance you choose to race, demands will be placed on you. You must weigh these demands against the race distance and finish time that you have set as a goal. You do not have to set a finish time for yourself, but doing so will help you to decide on minimum training requirements. Don't be afraid that this will take the fun out of competing in your first race—actually, it will help guarantee that you finish.

For the vast majority of us, triathlons are just a hobby or leisure-time activity. What's amazing, however, is that we can become so involved with our hobby. Your involvement with triathlons will go well beyond racing. Racing is only a small part of triathlons; training will occupy the majority of your workouts and will create the greatest demands on your time. Consider the following breakdown of triathlon training demands.

Physical

Endurance training is recognized as a part of a healthy lifestyle. However, the amount of training required to achieve good health is relatively small. Performing 20 min of continuous exercise three times a week at an intensity of 65% to 80% of your maximal heart rate is all that is really necessary.

To calculate your exercise intensity you need to know your resting and maximum heart rates. You usually measure your resting heart rate (RHR) when you first wake up in the morning, because this is when it tends to be its lowest. You may need to urinate first, because even mild stress can elevate your resting heart rate. To determine your maximum heart rate

(MHR), you must measure it. Predicting your maximum heart rate according to heart rate charts is not always accurate and should be avoided. For example, let's look at a commonly used formula, 220 − age = MHR, as applied to author Todd Kearney's mother. When Todd's mother was 61 years old, the formula predicted her MHR to be 159 beats per minute (BPM). Her actual maximum heart rate, achieved in a short race and recorded on a heart rate monitor, was 195 BPM—36 beats away from the formula prediction. Another formula, 209 − (age × .6) = MHR, given in the August 1991 issue of *Runner's World*, was also inaccurate for this particular woman; it predicted a value of 172 BPM.

Achieving your maximum heart rate is hard work. Some of you may have achieved your maximum heart rate sprinting to the finish line in a 5K or 10K running race. If you are over age 40, it is recommended that a physician be present as you attempt to reach your maximum heart rate. Maximum heart rate does not change with training. You have the same maximum heart rate whether you've spent the last 6 months as a "couch potato" or in serious training for an ultra event.

Twenty minutes of cardiovascular activity three times a week is considered a sufficient amount of aerobic exercise to maintain good health. Dr. Kenneth Cooper (considered by many the father of aerobic exercise) pointed out years ago that any exercise beyond this amount was driven by motives other than good health. Most multisport endurance athletes will admit that they work out for other reasons, such as earning a living. This can lead to excessive amounts of time spent on exercise. Too much exercise can actually destroy good health! In the long haul you have to practice moderation. Moderate exercise gives you more energy and decreases the stress you feel. Regular exercise is also the best way to manage your body weight.

Regular exercise does not protect you against injury, however. Moving the same muscles repeatedly leads to injury. Triathlon training helps you avoid injuries because you don't repeat the same muscle movements during every workout. This doesn't mean that you'll never get injured. Triathletes do experience injuries, but at a lower incidence than single-sport endurance athletes.

Financial

Simply put, training for three sports requires incurring the expenses of three sports. Even if you swim only once a week, you still need a swimsuit and goggles. Your longest bike ride may be only 15 mi, but you still need a dependable bike. The bicycle, in fact, will represent your greatest financial outlay. Bicycles are, technically speaking, the only piece of equipment a triathlete uses. But any run should be done wearing running shoes, which are not cheap. We'll explain the nature of these costs in detail in chapter 2.

Time

Although you might think that training for three sports at once would require as much time as training for three separate sports, this is not necessarily the case. The amount of time you spend training depends on what you want to accomplish, and what you accomplish is directly associated with the priorities you set. Different people set different priorities. Thinking about your priorities is essential to your success as a triathlete. Don't measure your success by how many races you win, but by the goals you've accomplished. To feel successful, you need to set and accomplish realistic goals. You'll use your time more efficiently.

Training takes up a considerable portion of your free time. Adding up the hours necessary for proper training to race in triathlons requires a number of calculations. Your totals have to include more than just the workouts. How about stretching, buying clothing and other items you need for your sport, and traveling to and from the places where you train and race? Consider 365 hr a year (an average of 1 hr each day) the minimum amount of time you need to train for an international distance triathlon. The ultra distance will require training about 20 hr a week. This is equivalent to using half your workday to train! If you think this seems like the vast majority of your total training time commitment, prepare yourself for more.

Stretching after your workouts can reasonably total about an hour each week. The more time you spend stretching, the better. Time spent buying clothing and other items might seem minor, but if you use your bicycle a lot, you'll spend about 3 to 4 hr a month to keep it in good repair. Travel time can vary widely, depending on whether you can work out at home or on the way to work, or if you have to go out of your way to get in your workout. A reasonable amount of time for travel is 30 min a day, or 3-1/2 hr each week. All of these reasonable time approximations add up to about 12 hr a week, or 635 hr a year—about 75% more time than you'll spend just working out. We aren't pointing all this out to discourage those of you who are new to triathlons, but we want to properly prepare you for the commitment you are considering.

Table 1.2 may help you decide what race distance you are willing to commit training time for. Certainly, some individuals will spend more time training than others, but these averages will give you a reasonable idea of what to expect.

Table 1.2
Estimated Weekly Training Times for Various-Distance Triathlons

Race distance	Training hr per week
Sprint	4–6 hr
International	7–10 hr
Long	10–14 hr
Ultra	14–40 hr

Social

This is an area the endurance athlete often overlooks. Your job can take up 40 to 80 hr a week of your time. Sleeping fills about another 56 hr. With 168 hr in a week, that leaves you about 30 to 70 hr to train. The more you use your free time for training, the less time you have to socialize with people not involved in training. In other words, the more you train, the more likely it is that your friends will be triathletes. People who are not associated with triathlon training will receive less and less of your time. This can be dangerous, especially if your significant others aren't very enthusiastic about triathlons. Note that the importance of training to one partner has been cited in the breakup of some marriages. You'll certainly make new friends as you become more involved with triathlons, but some of your established friends are going to think that you care more about triathlons than about them. This is why it is so crucial to determine how important training is to you.

If you've studied all the demands we've outlined and are still committed to becoming a triathlete, your next step is becoming well equipped for training and competition. Now it's important to decide what items are most important to you.

Chapter 2

Equipping Yourself

Determining your equipment and clothing needs depends as much on the size of your checkbook as it does on your personal tastes. The type of equipment and clothing you need to be a triathlete requires very difficult decisions. Of even greater importance to those of you who earn average incomes, however, is how much you can afford to spend on triathlon equipment and clothing. We will examine the mandatory and optional items that triathletes use in triathlon training and racing.

Another difficulty you'll face is finding a place to buy everything triathletes need. You may end up going to at least three different stores to find the items necessary for the three different sports. The larger the metropolitan area you live in, the better your chances of finding stores that cater to triathletes. If you live in an especially rural area, buying by mail order may be your only alternative.

Swimming

When selecting the clothing and equipment that you'll need for swimming, give equal consideration to what is comfortable as well as to what is functional. For example, swim trunks, although comfortable, will slow you down in the water because of the drag they produce. Most of the participants in sprint and international distance triathlons wear swimsuits for all three segments of the race—the swim, the bike, and the run. In fact, most female, and some male, triathletes race all distances in swimsuits. For triathlon training, however, you'll need to wear more than a swimsuit. The people in your community may not look favorably on your biking and running through town in such scanty attire.

A wide variety of equipment exists to help you build muscle strength, endurance, and stamina. When selecting equipment find someone to instruct you properly before using the equipment. If you have experienced, knowledgeable friends, ask them; otherwise seek out professionals for help.

W hen considering the cost of triathlon training, do not forget that you need to have a place to swim. A membership at a health club or the YMCA is another expense to consider. Be prepared to spend at least $200 a year for access to a swimming facility. Fortunately, this facility will probably provide you with other indoor training equipment as well, such as exercise bikes and weight machines.

Swimsuits

Men have little to worry about in selecting a suit, because there is not much variation in men's swimwear. The most important choice is whether to get a suit with a small pad in the crotch. The pad is not particularly useful for swimming, but it is for riding the bike. Riding for 40 km with no padding can be painful. Because you will not usually wear a swimsuit for bike training, this is a racing option.

With or without the pad, the suit should be made of a good quality fabric that can withstand regular use. This fabric is typically nylon, with varying percentages of Lycra added to it. The nylon provides durability (long wear), and the Lycra provides comfort (softer feel). This material dries quickly, does not easily tear, and is low in drag through both water and air. It is important to take good care of your suit. The chlorine used in swimming pools will cause the Lycra in your suit to deteriorate if you don't rinse out the suit with fresh water after each use. One other consideration is to look for a drawstring, preferably one that is longer than you think is needed. It's disheartening to pull off your suit only to find out that one of the ends of the drawstring has disappeared irretrievably into the waistband.

Women's swimsuits have a variety of backs (see Figure 2.1). Your particular body shape will determine which style feels more comfortable to you. As with men's suits, the material of choice for women's swimsuits is nylon with varying amounts of Lycra. Bustline support is an important consideration in buying a swimsuit that you will use for racing. Large-breasted women generally do not receive enough support from a swimsuit and wear a lightweight (typically nylon) sport bra underneath it. Women can also choose a two-piece suit that may provide more support and may prove to be more comfortable. In a two-piece suit, look for adequate material in the bottom to cover your gluteals and a top that has a sturdy elastic band under the bust. The choice between a one-piece and a two-piece suit is personal.

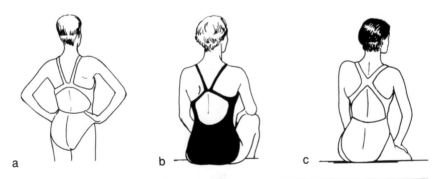

Figure 2.1   Three types of backs commonly available in women's swimsuits are the record breaker (a), the splashback (b), and the fusionback (c).

Wet Suits

Unless you plan to race exclusively in warm water, you should consider a wet suit. While a wet suit costs considerably more than the average swimsuit, it provides many benefits. The most obvious benefit is warmth. In cold-water swims (such as "The World's Toughest Triathlon" held at Lake Tahoe, Nevada) you are required to have a wet suit to participate.

Figure 2.2   Long john wet suit.

A wet suit also provides buoyancy. The effect of buoyancy places your body in a more horizontal position, and the closer you are to horizontal, the faster you swim (see chapter 3 for more information on swim biomechanics).

The following list describes the different types of wet suits.

- Shorty—sleeveless with short legs
- Long john—sleeveless with long legs (see Figure 2.2)
- Full—long sleeves and long legs

Obviously the shorty is the least expensive of the three and the full is the most expensive. Which one should you buy? Try to determine what the water temperature will be for the majority of your training and racing. If you will be training in a pool, consider what races you want to participate in. For water temperatures between 70 and 74 degrees choose a shorty. For water temperatures between 65 and 69 degrees choose a long john. For water temperatures below 65 degrees choose a full. If you will be in water of all temperature ranges, your best solution could be the middle ground, a long john.

Swim Caps

Swim caps come in four different materials: latex, Lycra, silicone, and neoprene. Almost every triathlon requires that racers wear swim caps to help lifeguards identify participants, and caps are usually provided in your race packet (see Figure 2.3). When provided, caps are usually mandatory. Latex caps are the most common type. They're the least expensive, but they do not last as long as the other types. Lycra caps do not pull your hair the way latex or silicone caps can, but they take longer to dry. If you use a Lycra cap in a pool, rinse out the chlorine as soon as possible afterward. Silicone caps are more durable but are also more expensive than latex caps. Cold-water swims (in water below 65 degrees) require a neoprene cap. This type is the most expensive, but if you swim in cold water, you'll need the warmth it provides.

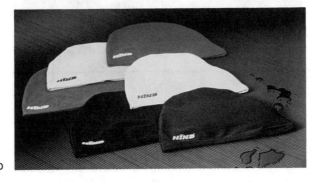

Figure 2.3 Swim caps: latex (a) and Lycra (b).

Goggles

There are many types of goggles to choose from. The greatest difference is in the shape of the lens. Some lenses are longer horizontally; others are closer to round (see Figure 2.4). Different shapes fit some people better than others. The only way you can find out if a particular style fits you is to try them on. A pair of goggles fit well if you feel even pressure all the way around your eye. Any gaps in the fit will allow water in. You also have a choice of lens colors. Clear lenses are best for indoor use; smoke-colored lenses are best for the outdoors. If you want to buy only one pair of goggles, decide whether you'll be indoors or outdoors most of the time. You'll probably want clear lenses. A good pair of goggles may cost more than twice as much as a cheaper pair. Don't buy cheap goggles if you feel they don't fit you well. Leaky goggles are a waste of your money!

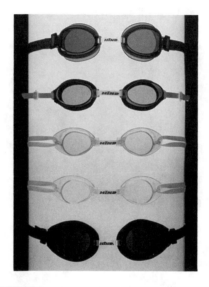

Figure 2.4   Swim goggles.

Fins

Fins are used in training to strengthen the legs and help you develop a powerful kick. You can purchase fins like shoes; they come in sizes. You can also purchase fins that are adjustable to different-sized feet. If you are going to be sharing your fins with anyone else, buy adjustable ones. Fins are not inexpensive; they will probably cost you twice as much as a good pair of goggles.

Hand Paddles

Using paddles in training strengthens the upper body and teaches you the correct hand positions for good biomechanics. They are not simply devices to create more resistance. Any object in or on your hand while you swim will make for higher resistance, but it will not train you for good hand positions. Paddles come in different shapes (see Figure 2.5), and each manufacturer claims that its design helps you to learn to swim better. The shape that will work best for you depends on the characteristics of your swimming stroke. This is difficult for you to determine without outside help. The paddles differ in size as well, because people are of varying sizes and strengths. A small person who is a weak swimmer will want to start with the smallest paddles available. A large person who is a strong swimmer will look for larger paddles.

Figure 2.5   Hand paddles and pull buoys.

Pull Buoys

A pull buoy is an optional device that you place between your legs to allow you to isolate the movement of your upper body from your legs (see Figure 2.5). Its highly buoyant material makes your legs and hips float, allowing you to concentrate on your arm movements during training (refer to chapter 3 for swim biomechanics). Pull buoys come in several different styles, all of which are comparable in efficiency. They come in different sizes, and you should choose one that is appropriate to your particular size.

Bicycling

You can spend a considerable amount of money on cycling clothing and equipment. The two "must-have" items are a bicycle and a helmet. The other items are helpful but not necessary. Because the majority of your training will take place on the bike, good clothing is important. Pressure on the hands and particularly the crotch make the average wardrobe insufficient for cycling. A trip to your local bicycle shop is essential; you will have a lot of choices to make.

Bicycles

Bicycles vary widely in cost. Remember, though, that an expensive bike will not necessarily make you faster. Concentrate on training your body to become a better cyclist. The additional money you spend on a bicycle should reflect increased dependability. Breakdowns will leave you frustrated and disappointed, especially if they occur during a race. When deciding what type is best for you, first consider the frame.

Frames.   Bicycle frames differ based on function. The different types of frames are a touring design, a road racing design, a hybrid of the two (called a "sport" frame), an off-road design (called an all-terrain bike [ATB] or mountain bike frame), a time-trial racing design, and a triathlon design.

Touring (see Figure 2.6) and mountain bike frames (see Figure 2.7) provide the cyclist with a more comfortable ride because the front forks are curved more at the ends (called fork rake). This allows for more road shock to be absorbed before you feel the vibrations in the hands. Although some mountain bikes use a straighter fork with shock absorbers, this type is not often used in triathlons. The head tube angle (forward pitch of the fork) is less than in racing frames, again minimizing road vibration. The gearing on a touring bike is designed to allow for a slow, steady ride with heavy loads on steeply graded roads. The gearing on a mountain bike includes three chain rings that are not necessary in a triathlon (more on gearing later). A mountain bike is likely to have T-shaped handlebars as opposed to the drop handlebars of a road racing bike, or the triathlon handlebars of a time-trial or triathlon bike. Some mountain bike racers use drop handlebars, but drop handlebars do not make a mountain bike a triathlon bike. The T handlebars enable you to maintain an erect, comfortable riding position but also create significant wind resistance. Mountain bikes are very popular, and you'll find plenty of them in bicycle shops.

Figure 2.6   Touring bike.

Figure 2.7   Mountain bike.

This will not be the frame you want to use to race in a triathlon, however. Although they're comfortable, there is a major tradeoff in performance.

The sport frame design (also called the cross or hybrid) (see Figure 2.8) emerged from the touring and the racing frame designs. There is some question as to whether this frame is effective in serving both touring and racing needs. Some believe the sport frame is for the overnight cycling tourist who needs frame strength to carry small loads but not the comfort required to cycle successive days of more than 100 miles each. Racing enthusiasts are attracted by the bike's medium weight and lower cost, but this frame compromises speed and responsiveness. This will probably not

Figure 2.8 Sport bike.

be the frame you want to use to race in a triathlon in that it sacrifices performance for comfort.

Consider instead the road racing frame (see Figure 2.9), the time-trial frame (see Figure 2.10), or the triathlon frame (see Figure 2.11). Designed to transfer all energies into a forward direction, these frames are your best choices for a triathlon bicycle. The fork is much straighter and the head tube angle is more vertical than in the bikes discussed previously. This design sacrifices shock absorbency and riding comfort, but the added stiffness allows more effort to be transferred to the wheels instead of being absorbed by the flexible frame. Also, the steeper angles create a difference in handling, making the racing frames less stable and more responsive. Interestingly, stability appreciably improves when speeds approach 20 mph.

The difference between the road racing frame and the time-trial frame is the size of the front wheel each holds. The road racing frame fits 27-in. (700c) front (and rear) wheels. The time-trial frame fits a 26-in. front wheel (while still using a 27-in. rear wheel; see Figure 2.10). This frame places the rider in an improved aerodynamic position.

The triathlon frame differs from the time-trial frame in two areas. First, the seat post of the triathlon frame may have a steeper angle (see Figure 2.11). This moves the rider further forward, into a position that can be called ''running on the pedals.'' This running position on the bike, though

Figure 2.9 Road bike.

Figure 2.10 Time-trial bike.

Figure 2.11 Triathlon bike.

it flies in the face of traditional cycling biomechanics, is highly effective for some triathletes (more on this later). The second difference is in the wheels. In triathlon bikes, both the front and rear wheels can be undersized. The energy cost to move a smaller wheel (24-in. or 26-in.) is less than to move a 27-in. wheel. However, the rolling resistance (amount of tire that contacts the ground, thereby producing friction) of the smaller wheel is greater than with the standard-size wheel. More research is needed before we can make a final recommendation on wheel size.

To sum it up, then, you need a frame design that will not require you to compromise performance; yet you do not want to be so stiff and sore after riding that you must be "unglued" from the bike.

Handlebars.   The road racing bicycle frame will likely come with drop handlebars. To reduce the drag from wind resistance, consider the aero handlebars now available. The simplest modification is clip-on aero handlebars (see Figure 2.12a). This is a nonpermanent step in that you can remove the clip-ons at any time. For a more permanent adjustment, use the full aero handlebars (see Figure 2.12b). This is a reasonable idea if

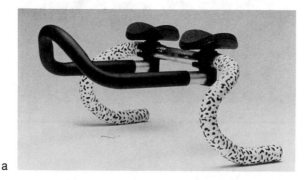

a

b

Figure 2.12   Clip-on aero handlebars (a) and full aero handlebars (b).

you are going to race only triathlons or time trials. If you plan to participate in any United States Cycling Federation races other than time trials, stay with the clip-ons. Aero handlebars are not allowed in criteriums (high speed, less than a mile loop, circuit races) or road races!

Aero handlebars have many advantages. The most important is the reduction of your frontal surface area, which creates a knifelike effect that enables you to slice through the wind. The other benefit of aero handlebars is the comfort derived from placing your body weight on your forearms instead of on your hands. This position also relaxes the back and neck muscles. The cost is about $100—we think it's money well spent.

Components.   Now that we've dealt with the performance-related (and usually the most expensive) considerations involved in developing your triathlon bike, let's look at components that can improve your bike's reliability, although they have very little effect on performance and rolling resistance. Reliability means two things: the ability to stand up to the many stresses that cyclists demand (durability), and the ability to perform year after year (wearability). Consider durability and wearability when purchasing the drive train, brakes, stem, and bars. A chain lighter in weight may break more easily. The gears on your bike may wear down more quickly if they are made of a lightweight, but cheap, material. Bike shops seldom carry low- or medium-quality replacement parts.

T he correct term for the gears on the front of your bicycle is *chain rings*. Forty-two-tooth and 52-tooth chain rings are normal on road racing bicycles. The correct term for the gears on the back of your bicycle is *cogs*. The smallest cog is likely to have 12 teeth; the largest cog probably will have 24 teeth but can have as many as 32 teeth.

Manufacturers have given much attention to aerodynamics in creating frames and components. They've made teardrop-shaped frame tubes, routed shift and brake cables through the frame, and constructed frames of space-age materials. Scientists suggested in 1983 that a rider must overcome 3.27 lb of force to maintain a 20-mph speed on an aerodynamically equipped bike, compared to 3.48 lb of force on a bike without aerodynamic modifications. (This calculation assumes the same riding position on equally weighted bikes with the same tires and tire pressure.)

The difference reflects an approximately 6% greater efficiency from using an aerodynamically equipped bike. Although this difference is worth noting, the real cycling economies come from the position you maintain on the bike.

Wheels and Tires

Unfortunately, nothing on a bicycle is streamlined. The wind drag of certain cycle components and accessories can affect your performance. Table 2.1 shows the wind drag of certain cycle components and accessories at 20 mph.

Together, the wheels and tires are the components that can most affect the bike's riding characteristics, cornering ability, load-carrying tasks, acceleration, and efficiency as reflected in minimal rolling resistance. Use Table 2.2 to find the total resistance force. Multiply the rolling-resistance coefficient (*CRR*) by the total weight.

Hubs.   Triathletes are now finding good success with hubs having fewer than the standard 36 spokes. With a 28- to 32-spoke hub, for instance, the fewer spokes create less wind resistance and are lighter. Scientists Kyle and Zahradnik found that this type of spoke configuration will save

Table 2.1

The Aerodynamic Drag of Cycle Components and Equipment: The Effect of Rider Position and the Drag of Cycle Helmets

Cycle components and helmets	Relative drag
Cycle components—speed 20 mph	
Bare cycle rider in straight-armed racing position	0 (reference)
Rider in crouched racing position	−.65 lb (−20%)
Rider in hill-descent position	−.94 lb (−29%)
Cycle plus water bottle	+.10 lb
Cycle plus fenders	+.28 lb
Cycle plus paniers and packs	+.60 lb
Cycle with frame and wheels covered with stretched plastic	−.20 lb
Helmets—speed 30 mph	
Rider with long hair	0 (reference)
Rider plus Cinelli Stap helmet	−.13 lb
Rider plus Brancale helmet	−.26 lb
Best—rider plus aero helmet	
Worst—rider with long hair	

Table 2.2
The Rolling Resistance of Bicycle Tires on a Smooth Surface

Tire type	Drag	Weight on tire	CRR
20 × 2-1/4 in. 45 psi Knobby Tires BMX	2.74 lb	163 lb	.017
27 × 2-1/4 in. 45 psi Knobby Tires BMX	2.27 lb	175 lb	.013
18 × 1-1/4 in. 120 psi Road Sew-ups 160 g	1.01 lb	194.4 lb	.0052
20 × 1-1/4 in. 120 psi Road Sew-ups 180 g	0.88 lb	195 lb	.0045
27 × 1-1/8 in. 95 psi Road Clinchers	0.78 lb	199 lb	.0039
24 × 1-1/8 in. 120 psi Road Sew-ups 200 g	0.73 lb	196 lb	.0037
27 in. × 18 mm 120 psi Road Sew-ups 160 g	0.67 lb	196.2 lb	.0034
17-1/4 in. 90 psi Road Clinchers-Moulton	0.68 lb	204.2 lb	.0034
17-1/4 in. 120 psi Road Clinchers-Moulton	0.58 lb	204.2 lb	.0028
27 × 1 in. 120 psi Road Sew-ups 180 g	0.58 lb	178.5 lb	.0033
27 in. × 18 mm 120 psi Track Sew-ups 80–110 g	0.30–0.50 lb	193.6 lb	.0016–.0026

106 g of drag at 30 mph. Wheels exist with as few as 13 spokes (the minimum International Cycling Federation legal limit). Riding on fewer spokes than standard is not a good idea for someone who weighs 170 lb or more. Fewer spokes create a more fragile wheel.

One final decision confronting you in choosing hubs is whether to get sealed bearing hubs. Sealed bearing hubs are designed to require less maintenance, which may also allow you to use the hubs longer before replacing them. The tradeoff, however, is rolling resistance. A definite compromise exists in rolling resistance between sealed and standard bearing hubs. At the bike shop, turn the spindles of the two different types for comparison and then judge for yourself. Consider using sealed bearing hubs if you find yourself frequently training in the rain or on dusty, windy roads. Otherwise, stick with standard bearing hubs and enjoy maximum efficiency.

Spokes.   There are many types of spokes. You can choose between double-butted (spokes that get thinner in the middle), straight-gauge, and bladed ones. Straight-gauge spokes are the same diameter throughout. Kyle and Zahradnik found that substituting bladed spokes for straight gauge spokes saved 0.6 g of drag for every spoke replaced. Choose straight-gauge spokes if you weigh more than approximately 170 lb, are capable of applying great torque, or find yourself on rough roads. Otherwise, reduce drag and go with double-butted or bladed spokes.

You do not have to use wheels with standard spokes. Disk wheels and composite wheels are popular (but expensive) alternatives. These wheels have become popular because they improve performance by lessening the drag coefficient of the bicycle. The reduction in drag comes from the elimination of the spokes. Each spoke of your wheel has to cut through the wind and faces resistance when doing so. With a solid wheel area, the disk wheel has only to fight wind resistance as a whole. Although the drag of one spoke is small, multiple spokes produce a cumulative effect. The sum of the drag of the spokes is greater than the drag of the disk. Kyle and Zahradnik found that a disk wheel can save more than 130 g of drag at 30 mph. This translates into savings of 49 sec in a 40-km (24.8-mi) race. Note that the disk wheel is not lighter than a spoked wheel. The improved performance results completely from the drag reduction.

The drawback to the disk wheel is instability in a crosswind. The solid wheel area acts as a sail, catching the wind and making handling difficult. This is especially true when a disk wheel is on the front of the bicycle. The front wheel is responsible for the handling of the bicycle. To alleviate handling problems, most triathletes use a disk wheel only on the rear.

The composite wheel (also known as the tri-spoke, quad-spoke, or quint-spoke) has the advantage of reducing drag like the disk wheel yet maintaining the handling characteristics of the standard-spoke wheel. This makes it an excellent (but expensive) choice for the triathlete. The bike shown in Figure 2.11 is equipped with composite wheels.

An aerodynamic wheel generally costs over $300 and can be as much as $800. That is a lot of money. The time savings is more than 3 min for a person doing a 40-km time trial in 60 min. That is a large time savings, but unless it will move you up to the top three finishers in your age group, don't consider this an essential purchase.

You are going to spend a lot of money if you decide to use 26-in. wheels—not because the wheels cost so much, but because they won't fit on your standard road bike. One word of caution: The results are not conclusive that 26-in. wheels are faster than disk or composite-spoke wheels.

Rims.   Selecting a rim can be very difficult if you do not have a specific purpose in mind. Before choosing a rim, you must make a major decision as to which of the two types of tire and tube systems to use: clinchers or tubulars.

Clinchers are the more conventional design. The tire is separate from the tube and is held to the rim by mating the wire circumference of the tire over the metal bead on the rim. The tube consumes space in the tire and rim and when inflated keeps the wire from popping off the rim. In the past, racers thought clinchers were of poor quality. The tires were big and heavy, carried low-inflation ratings (meaning more drag due to increased rolling resistance), and were simply lacking in performance. Because the clincher system also provided some excellent qualities (such as lower cost and easy repair), however, designers began creating smaller, lighter, and higher (inflation) pressure styles. Manufacturers now consider clincher tire performance to be equal in performance to tubular tires.

With tubular tires, the tire and tube are inseparable. The tire casing completely encompasses the tube, and the casing walls are then sewn together. For this reason, tubular tires are often called *sew-ups*. The tubular rim in cross section is concave to receive the convex curvature of the tire. Proper mating of the tire to the rim is important to prevent the tire from shifting or rolling off during fast, tight turns. A special glue is used to accomplish this mating. Figure 2.13 illustrates the design differences between the two tire systems. These design differences enable us to compare the advantages and disadvantages of the two systems. Table 2.3 categorizes these comparisons.

In addition to deciding between clinchers and tubulars, you must also contend with rim width, strength, and weight. You should attempt to match your body weight to rim weight.

Next, you need to decide how important rolling resistance is to you. If you are seeking the path of least rolling resistance, opt for tubular rims. If you want a simpler system, consider working with a narrow clincher rim. The rim should be of an aero design (except for heavier riders). These rims should be no more than 19 to 20 mm wide; wider rims will not accept the newer narrow-profile tires that claim to provide minimal rolling resistance.

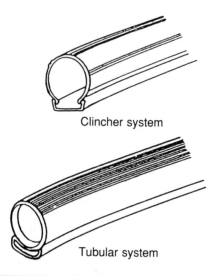

Clincher system

Tubular system

Figure 2.13   Clincher and tubular systems.

Table 2.3
Advantages and Disadvantages of the Different Rim Systems

Tubulars	Clinchers
1. More expensive	1. Less expensive
2. Time-consuming to patch	2. Easy to patch
3. Requires glueing	3. More prone to flats from spokes and tire irons
4. Less availability	4. Readily available
5. Fast and easy to change	5. Slightly harder to change a flat
6. Overall a lighter system	6. Slightly heavier system
7. Can take higher tire pressures	7. Slightly more rolling resistance
8. Superior handling and traction	8. Satisfactory handling and traction

In advertisements that followed the 1991 professional cycling year, manufacturers claimed that clinchers had achieved parity with tubulars and that the top stars of cycling had switched to clinchers in major stage races. This was partially true, because the stars did use clinchers throughout most of the races. Stage races take many days to complete, and only a few of these days are time trial races. During the time trial race days, however, the stars reverted to tubulars!

Whichever rim and tire system you choose, make sure you run the tires at the proper inflation. Scientists Faria and Cavanagh found that underinflated tires increased rolling resistance about 12% for every 20-lb reduction in inflation pressure. An underinflated tire not only is inefficient, it is also dangerous. Low-profile tires require optimal inflation to elevate the rim off the road's surface. Soft tires allow for the tire and tube to be pinched between the rim and a bump or debris on the road. A blowout, a bent rim, or both can result when the tube is pinched between the tire and the rim.

Most of the energy you lose in cycling comes from fighting wind resistance. Overcoming the rolling resistance of the tires creates an additional energy loss. Rolling resistance occurs because of the deformation or flattening of the tire, the wheel, and the riding surface. Your pedaling motion provides the energy needed for both movement and deformation. Loss of energy results when the wheel, tire, and road surface do not return the energy required to deform them. Here are two ways to tell that energy has been lost. Feel your tires after you have ridden. Are they warm? This is because of deformation energy. Also, when you leave a rut in soft ground you have used energy.

The rolling resistance of bicycle tires is nearly constant. If they use the same tires, cyclists of all levels of ability have to deal with the same amount of drag. The following factors will reduce rolling resistance: larger diameter wheels (remember that this increases air resistance), narrower tires, and less weight on the wheels.

Helmets

No option here, helmets are mandatory in all triathlons. That's because helmets save lives! You can choose any helmet that is approved by the American National Standard Institute (ANSI) or Snell (their ratings reflect the helmet's ability to withstand a crash). The more expensive aerodynamic helmets (costing probably twice as much as a normal helmet) will save you about 6 sec in a 40-km race, but not much more. An important consideration is the helmet's coolness rating. Look for a bicycle magazine with helmet reviews to find coolness ratings. They do not appear in the helmet. Because you generate considerable amounts of heat when exercising, you want to be able to stay cool.

H elmets are an integral part of bicycle riding. Because all triathlons require helmets, you should consider the following factors
before you make your purchase.

- What is the helmet's ANSI or Snell rating? The higher the
  rating, the harder the crash your head is going to survive. This
  is important.
- What is the coolness rating of the helmet? Some helmets that
  look cool might not have the proper rating to keep your head
  cool in the heat of racing.
- How about the weight of the helmet? Expect to pay more for
  a helmet that weighs less than normal. Most likely, a couple
  of extra ounces will not strain your neck on anything but the
  longest rides.
- How concerned are you with aerodynamics? Expect to pay
  more for any helmet designed to cut drag to a minimum.

Sunglasses

Given the high speeds you attain when cycling, eyewear is an important
safety consideration. Ultraviolet protection is a standard feature in all
good-quality glasses. High-impact resistance is also important and is often
lacking in cheaper sunglasses. Some manufacturers make vent holes in
the lenses to help prevent fogging, but this costs more. The weather
conditions will dictate whether you need this option. In high humidity,
your glasses will likely fog up with any type of lens and running increases
this effect. Ask other triathletes to recommend the brands they prefer.

Cyclecomputer

A cyclecomputer can monitor a variety of functions, such as your speed,
average speed, maximum speed, total miles, trip miles, elapsed time,
clock, cadence, even altitude. A cyclecomputer will not make you faster,
but it will provide you with valuable feedback during and after your rides.
It is truly an item worth having. If the cost is prohibitive, check around
for a used one.

Water Bottles

Considering the importance of staying hydrated and the low cost of water bottles and water bottle cages, this is an easy purchase for you to make. Aerodynamic water bottles and cages aren't worth the extra money; they won't save you that much time.

Pumps

There are two types of pumps, floor and frame. A frame pump is roughly the same size as the top tube of your bike, and this is usually the place you attach it. A frame pump saves you when you get a flat on the road. A floor pump enables you to properly inflate your tires at the beginning of your workout. A floor pump can inflate tires to higher pressures and do the job in less time. Neither pump is overly expensive, but you've accumulated quite a shopping list by this point, so get the frame pump first; after all, you need to be able to get back home after a flat.

Shorts

Bicycle shorts are the single most important piece of clothing for long rides. Though they are expensive, the pain or numbness you'll experience on a long ride without them makes their cost a lot easier to bear. They are made mostly of nylon and Lycra, materials that last a long time. Bicycle shorts fit snugly; if you are not used to tight clothing, let a salesperson help you with the fit. The better manufacturers offer separate men's and women's designs that are padded differently. Take advantage of the anatomical design differences.

Jerseys

For clothing the upper body during cycling, we recommend a jersey. You may be comfortable wearing a T-shirt or something lighter for riding, but consider these options. Jerseys are made with a short or long sleeve. The sleeve is a practical idea—it protects your shoulders if you fall. United States Cycling Federation (USCF) races require participants to wear shirts with sleeves. Jerseys are made with back pockets to hold food and water bottles. You may find these pockets valuable on long rides. Jerseys are usually made of nylon and Lycra. Because nylon is not particularly absorbent, you may find a cotton jersey more comfortable.

Jerseys are not required in triathlons, but consider them for long races or for training. Although they're expensive, they are of high quality and last for a long time. They fit snugly, and you may want some help in choosing one if you're not used to tight-fitting clothing.

Gloves

Wearing gloves helps relieve the pressure associated with riding on the drops (lowest point of the handlebars) or hoods (tops of the break levers) of your handlebars. They also protect your hands when you crash and enable you to clean road glass and gravel from your tires while you're in motion. (We will discuss this aspect of maintenance later in this chapter.) In cold weather, gloves with full fingers provide warmth. The cost of cycling gloves is relatively small compared to that of other bicycle accessories, so think of them as an important item to add to your wardrobe.

Shoes

You can use running shoes for riding, but you'll lose energy through flexing the soles. A cycling shoe has a stiff sole, which transfers the energy generated by your body more efficiently to the bicycle. The soft sole of a running shoe flexes when you apply pressure down on the pedal. This results in less efficient energy transfer.

The nearly permanent connection of the cleated cycling shoe to the pedal is a drawback. It's quite difficult to get your foot out of a toe clip and cleated shoe combination quickly. The result can be disastrous, especially if you are trying to come to a complete stop. Cycling shoes are not cheap, but they last a long time. Consider this a valuable investment, not just an option.

Pedals

The triathlete must choose from many combinations of pedals and shoes. The first step in the evolution of pedal and shoe combinations was toe clips (also called cages) and cleated cycling shoes (see Figure 2.14).

Standard equipment on most road bikes are regular pedals, which are called cages. Cages use toe straps (leather or plastic material used to tighten the toe clip around the shoe), that release the shoe only with a hand release. This drawback led to the development of the clipless pedal (see Figure 2.15). In this system, the cycling shoe uses a cleat that adapts

Figure 2.14   Cleated cycling shoes.

Figure 2.15   Clipless pedals.

to the shape of a slot in the pedal. If you are interested in a more functional pedal system, then you need to consider clipless pedals. These are likely to cost you more when buying a bike, but they provide solid foot-to-pedal contact, not the vice grip associated with regular pedals. Clipless pedals use ski binding technology and allow you to release your shoe with a twisting motion. This option is becoming more affordable every year. Clipless pedals provide better aerodynamics—a 20-g reduction in drag compared to toe clips. Cycling experts Kyle and Zahradnik translated this into an 8-sec savings in a 40-km race, described in their June 1987 *Bicycling* article, "Aerodynamic Overhaul."

All these pedal and shoe advancements have helped cyclists as well as triathletes. But triathletes (and especially duathletes) have an additional concern: How do you get into and out of your cycling shoes and pedals quickly? To a competitive multisport athlete, the transition on and off the bike is important. A slow transition will cost you a considerable amount of time. The distance of the race determines how important this concern is to the triathlete. It is most important to sprint distance competitors and less of a concern to ultra athletes. The *transition* pedal and shoe system was designed to reduce transition time (see Figure 2.16). The cyclist uses a running shoe with a pedal containing a platform that provides the stiff base normally provided by a cycling shoe.

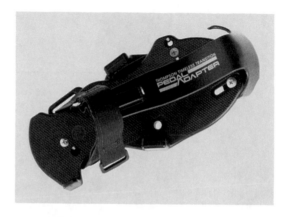

Figure 2.16   Thompson Timeless Transition pedal.

Stationary Trainers

In inclement weather, your only choice may be to cycle indoors. Bicycling is too important a component of a triathlon for you to go for days without training. A variety of stationary trainers are on the market with basic models ranging from $100 to $250. Look for something that holds your bicycle solidly so as to prevent damage to the frame from vibration and sway. Whether it holds the bike at the seat post, rear axle, or front fork does not matter as much as whether it provides a secure hold.

Options include resistance provided by a fan unit (which provides for cooling but is noisier) or by a magnet unit (which is quieter but does not provide cooling). The most extravagant stationary trainers simulate hills and different race courses. Expect to pay considerably more for these options.

Fitting Your Body to the Machine

Unless you can afford to have a frame custom built to your specific anatomy, your next step should be to make customized adjustments to your bicycle. As you purchase various components to build up your bike, be prepared to specify thread design, seat post diameter, and some components based on your body's various physical dimensions. Four bike parts require you to know your body size before you make your purchase. These are the frame size, the length of the crank arms, the stem length, and possibly the toe clips.

Frame Size. You can use several techniques to determine the proper frame size for your body (see Table 2.4). Store clerks usually have you straddle the top tube, and when the clearance between your crotch and the top tube measures about an inch, the frame size is correct. This method, however, fails to consider differences in wheel and tire size and ground clearance of the bottom bracket, which could lead to a sizing error of as much as 2 in. Determine frame size based on your leg length. De la Rosa and Kolin suggested in their book *The Ten-Speed Bicycle* (1979) the following technique:

> Measure the distance from the greater trochanter of the femur
> to the floor (in bare feet). Subtract 13.75 inches (34 centimeters)
> from that measurement to determine the correct frame size.

Table 2.4
Determining Frame Size

Method	Measured by	Advantage	Disadvantage
Store clerk	Straddling the top tube	Easy	Frequently gives errors of 2 in. or more
De la Rosa and Kolin	Subtracting 13.75 in. from the length of the greater trochanter to the floor	Gives accurate results	Many people do not accurately locate the greater trochanter
Van der Plas	Subtracting 10.5 in. from your inseam	Easy	May yield low results
LeMond	Multiplying your inseam by 0.833	Easy	May yield high results

Van der Plas (1986) suggested subtracting 10.5 in. from your inseam measurement to determine the appropriate frame size. LeMond (1987) recommended multiplying your inseam measurement by 0.833 for proper sizing.

Next, position the saddle for proper height, tilt, and front-to-back position. When properly adjusted, the saddle's surface will be horizontal or tilted slightly up at the neck. Saddle height is a very important concern because it greatly influences your mechanical efficiency and injury potential. Hamley and Thomas (1967) pointed out that every 4% change in saddle height can affect power output by approximately 5%. Saddle heights that are too high or too low can wreak havoc with your knees. (We discuss knee injuries in chapter 10.) Researchers Shennum and deVries (1976) suggested a practical technique for approximating the ideal saddle height. Stand upright wearing cycling shoes. Place your feet 12 in. apart, then measure from the floor to your crotch. Take this value and multiply it by 1.09. This represents the distance from the pedal axle to the top of the seat as shown in Figure 2.17.

Realize that your individual physical characteristics may require you to make some small adjustments from this setting. Whatever saddle height you set, be careful that your hips do not drop with each spin of the pedal. If your hips rock from side to side, the saddle height is too high.

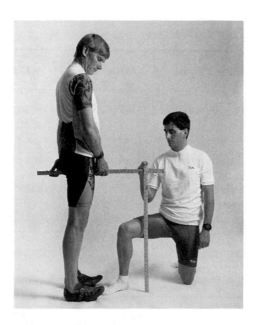

Figure 2.17   Measurement needed in determining correct frame size.

Most saddles have rail mounts that allow you to move the saddle forward and back about 3 in. Make this adjustment while sitting on the saddle, with your feet in the toe clips and the pedal crank arms horizontal to the ground. Position the saddle so that the center of your front knee falls no further back than through the center of the pedal. Many multisport athletes prefer a forward position, and manufacturers have designed seat posts that move the saddle forward. A string taped to the center of your knee and weighted on the other end will help you make a more exact measurement. Figure 2.18 demonstrates a technique for proper saddle adjustment.

Figure 2.18   Forward and backward adjustment of the saddle.

Length of Crank Arms.   Crank arms differ in length, ranging from 165 to 180 mm. The longer the crank arm, the higher your foot will be at top dead center (TDC, or the 12 o'clock position) and the lower your foot will be at bottom center (or 6 o'clock). Longer crank arms produce more power, *if* the same force is applied as to shorter crank arms. That's a big if, because in cycling, you can exert your optimal muscular strength over only a limited range of motion.

A crank arm that is too long can be as detrimental to your mechanics as having your saddle height too high. If you are 6-ft tall or taller, use crank arms of 175 mm or longer. If you are 5- to 6-ft tall, the standard size cranks of 170 mm should be used. If you are less than 5-ft tall, consider cranks of 165 mm.

Stem Length (Fitting the Upper Body).   All the adjustments we've discussed to this point have involved fitting your lower body to the bike. Your upper body characteristics will affect your selection of correct handlebar stem length, the stem height, and the pitch of the handlebars. Ideally, you could ask your bike dealer to determine proper stem length by using an adjustable stem. Stem adjustment can get very technical; racers use this measurement to distribute their body weight on each wheel, allowing for a more horizontal position. The triathlete needs a stem length that will allow for a comfortable position. If the stem length is too short, you'll be in too upright a position (causing poor aerodynamics); if it's too long, you'll be too stretched out on the bike. Make this adjustment with your hands on the flat portion of the handlebars, called the drops, and your wrists straight. If you have aero handlebars you can make the stem height adjustment in the aero position. Stem height should be about 1 in. lower than the top of the saddle (see Figure 2.19).

Stem designs allow for adjustments in the handlebar pitch. The drops should be pointing downhill. When the pitch is properly adjusted, your wrists will come directly down onto the drops without having to bend.

Figure 2.19   Setting proper seat height measurement and horizontal adjustment of the saddle.

Securing the Feet.   The next step is to secure your foot properly into the pedals. Minimum equipment for this effort is toe clips. You can improve this function by adding cleated cycling shoes to your cycling gear (see Figure 2.14) as well as clipless pedals (see Figure 2.15) or transition pedals (see Figure 2.16). If you cannot immediately afford cycling shoes, we recommend that you make some changes in your lifestyle until you save the money; they are that important. Toe clips come in small, medium, and large sizes based on shoe size. Cycling shoes must fit the foot snugly yet be free enough to keep the foot from cramping. When the cleat is properly adjusted, the ball of the foot is directly over the pedal axle. The inside heel of the foot should clear the crank arm by approximately a quarter of an inch.

The Modified Road Racing Frame

If you want to make a road racing frame more of a triathlon bike, consider the following modifications to enhance both performance and comfort. First, check the length of the handlebar stem. In the typical road racing bicycle this stem is quite long, allowing the racer to stretch out his or her body. Racing in this position is more aerodynamic, and it also places the hip extensor muscles in a better position to apply pedal force. This position is fine for racing, but being stretched out for so long can make it difficult for you to get off your bike and complete the run segment that follows in a triathlon. So, consider stem modification. A shorter stem will allow you a more upright position, which will give you a chance to do well in the run.

C onsider this rule of thumb for determining stem length when using drop handlebars. Assume a riding position on the bike. Look down through the top of the handlebar stem. You should see the front axle approximately 2 in. above the handlebar stem.

Next, check the racing saddle on your bicycle. If you have an inflexible saddle, consider replacing it with a padded racing or gel (a thick fluid enclosed in a sac under the top layer of material) saddle.

Padding the drop handlebars can also increase comfort. We have found the Spenco grips to be the best. Wearing riding gloves can add extra padding to all types of grips.

Let's now decide how to complete your frame. Some of the terminology can get technical, so use Figure 2.20 to aid you in identifying the components being discussed. We will talk about wheels and tires, handlebars, pedals and shoes, and components to help you decide what you want on your bicycle. Table 2.5 gives an accurate guide on the costs of "speeding up" your bike.

Preventive Maintenance

Mechanical problems can arise any time in training and competition, but you can do several things to minimize these occurrences. The number-one nemesis of cyclists is the flat tire. The best way to minimize this problem is to train on roads that are in good condition. High-performance tires are just not built to withstand the abuse of chuckholes, garbage on the pavement, and the like.

Another technique to avoid flats is to clean off your tires after going through loose gravel or passing over glass. As mentioned previously, this

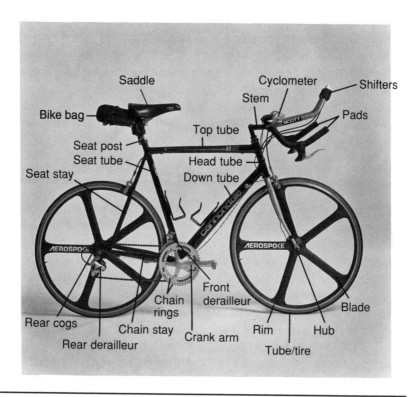

Figure 2.20 Bicycle parts.

Table 2.5
Aero Economics

Item	Time savings	Typical cost	Cost per second
1. Aero bars	3 min 21 sec	$ 65.00	$ .32
2. Aero bar-end shifters	1 min 40 sec	50.00	.50
3. Aero drinking system	30 sec	20.00	.67
4. Aero helmet	51 sec	90.00	1.76
5. 18 mm tires (air pressure 150 psi)	16 sec	50.00	3.13
6. Deep-rim front wheel	1 min 4 sec	360.00	5.63
7. Disc wheel	58 sec	580.00	10.00

Note. Maximum time savings on a 40-km bike course (riding at 25 mph).

is where cycling gloves come in handy. While in motion, lightly rub the reinforced palm over the rolling surface of the front tire. For the back tire, place your palm just behind the seat tube, lower it onto the rear tire, and rub it lightly. Don't be surprised to see glass fly off when you do this. Finally, do not ride on tires with worn treads. Not only is this unsafe, but by doing so, you're just begging for a flat.

If your bike is well maintained, tire repair should be your only concern when riding. If you ride on clinchers, carry one spare tube, two tire irons, and a patch kit. All this equipment can easily fit under your seat, allowing you to forget about it until the need arises. If you ride on tubulars, all you need are two spares. In either case, having some change tucked away somewhere can come in handy in case you have to phone for help.

Probably the next biggest concern in bike maintenance relates to the chain. Your chain will stretch, and over time it will play havoc with the teeth on both your chain rings and rear cogs. When this happens count on spending $10 for chain replacement and another $80 to replace all your gears. Measuring is the best way to tell if your chain has stretched too much. If 12 links measure 12 in., your chain is fine. However, if 12 links measure 12-1/8 in. or more, your chain is stretched and needs replacing.

It's a good idea to keep two chains on hand. While riding on one, soak the other in solvent so it is clean and ready to go when it's time to switch. The time to change your chain depends on your environment; change it if you get caught in the rain or ride on a very windy day. Just one day like this is enough to push dirt into your chain. If weather conditions are good, then lubricate the chain on your bike with a chain-lubricating spray.

Lubricating your chain is very important. A well-lubricated chain is perfectly silent as it functions. Any chain noise at all should signal you that it needs attention. When you rivet your chain back on, you must loosen up any stiff links. If you forget this measure, you'll experience the frustration of a skipping chain.

Getting caught in the rain presents some other maintenance problems as well, because your bike is probably made of steel, which can rust, and your bearings have grease that is harmed by dirt and water (even if the grease manufacturer claims it's waterproof). After getting caught in the rain once or twice, you'll need to dismantle all moving parts not containing sealed bearings and let the frame dry out before reassembling. This requires some additional shop equipment such as a crank arm extractor, but the cost is less than that of replacing parts ruined by dirt and rust.

Something we can't emphasize enough is the importance of doing your own bicycle maintenance. You should be able to change a broken spoke, true a wheel (make sure it is round and straight), change a chain, and maintain your headset (steering column) and bottom bracket (where the crank axle goes through). Tools to perform all these functions will cost about $60; in addition, plenty of excellent books on the subject are available. Popular books such as *The Ten-Speed Bicycle* by de la Rosa and Kolin (1979) or Sloan's *The New Complete Book of Bicycling* (1970) can guide you through the maintenance of your entire bicycle. Other maintenance measures you should perform on a less frequent basis include inspecting your rims for their trueness, checking your brake pads for wear, and checking your derailleurs for proper adjustment. A well-maintained, good-quality bicycle is remarkably reliable and a sheer joy to ride.

Running

Your checkbook may show a pretty low balance by this point, but you'll need a few more critical items for running. The first is shoes. Of the three sports in the triathlon, running carries the highest risk of injury. A good pair of shoes goes a long way in protecting you from injury. The other items we mention will be useful, but you can decide whether you really need them.

Shoes

Because running accounts for the majority of the injuries triathletes sustain during training, your need for a good pair of running shoes is critical. Tennis or aerobic shoes will not do; they are designed for the lateral motions involved in moving (such as from one side of the court to the other) or doing jumping jacks, not for the impact associated with running. Running does not require the lateral motion protection built into other types of sport shoes. It is a straight-ahead, heelstrike type of movement. A runner's heelstrike produces a force many times that of his or her body weight. Continually subjecting your body to this kind of force without protection raises the injury risk. Running shoes should provide exceptional cushioning for your heel.

Running shoes have many features to protect you from impact with the ground. Each year these features become more sophisticated. Here are a few things you should determine before selecting a running shoe.

1. Determine your degree of pronation. Pronation is the inward movement or rotation of your foot as it strikes the ground, when your ankle appears to bow slightly inward during contact. It occurs when the arch of your foot flattens as a result of bearing your weight. Pronation is normal and necessary. Without it your body would be unable to absorb much shock, and you'd be confined to running on ideal surfaces. Overpronation, or hyperpronation, is an excessive rotation and can lead to greater stress on the ligaments, tendons, and muscles of the lower body. Underpronation, or lack of rotation, can lead to a number of foot injuries and possibly other lower body injuries.

You can usually tell if you over- or underpronate by looking at an old pair of your running shoes as they sit on a flat surface, like a table. If your shoes lean inward you are likely an overpronator (see Figure 2.21a). You should wear a running shoe with a firmer midsole and motion control. If your shoes lean outward you are likely an underpronator (see Figure 2.21b). You should get a highly cushioned shoe. If your shoes appear to sit relatively straight, you are a normal pronator (see Figure 2.21c). You have a wide choice of shoes to select from.

2. Determine your foot structure. This is not difficult to do. Some shoe stores have you stand on pressure-sensitive film to make an impression of your foot. Or you can stand on a piece of paper (try a piece of a grocery bag) with wet feet. If you leave a full footprint you have a low arch (see Figure 2.22a). You will need a straight or possibly slightly curved shoe. You are also likely to be an overpronator. This means that you need a shoe with a firm midsole and motion control. If you leave little in the way of a footprint, especially in the middle of your foot, you have a high arch (see Figure 2.22b). You will need a curved shoe. You are also likely to be an underpronator. This means that you should get a highly cushioned shoe. If you leave a normal arch pattern, you can choose from all shoe shapes (see Figure 2.22c).

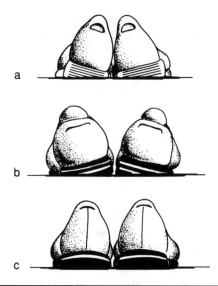

Figure 2.21 You can see the excessive rotation of the foot in the inside wear on the shoes (a). Lack of rotation is apparent when shoes wear on the outside (b). Normal rotation is evident when there is even wear on the shoes (c).

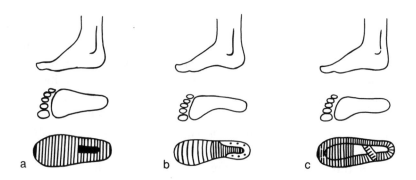

Figure 2.22 Runners with flat feet need a shoe with a straight shape (a). Runners with high arches benefit from a curved shoe with a lot of midsole cushioning (b). Runners with moderate arches can wear a variety of shoes with a slightly curved shape (c).

3. Determine your body size. Men weighing over 160 to 170 lb should wear a heavier shoe. You are producing great force with each footstrike. A heavier shoe will provide more protection. Men under 140 lb might consider a women's shoe. Your foot could be narrower than the standard men's shoe, and you might not need the weight a men's shoe provides.

Women over 140 to 150 lb should consider wearing a men's shoe. Your foot could be wider than the standard women's shoe, and you could benefit from the protection. Not all men's and women's shoes are available in the opposite sexes. Talk to your running shoe store salesperson for advice.

A few of the running shoe options available can make running more comfortable for you. Consider the following items when you're selecting a pair of shoes.

- A notch in the back of the heel collar prevents irritation of the Achilles tendon.
- An external heel counter provides additional support and controls overpronation.
- A forefoot-stability strap, made of either leather or plastic and over-laying both sides of the midfoot area, reinforces the upper part of the shoe. It also provides stability and support.

Training. Training shoes are made to absorb the force produced from footstrikes in your everyday training runs (see Figure 2.23). Made of materials that do a good job of protecting you, these shoes may seem relatively heavy compared to other athletic shoes you own. They may also, unfortunately, seem quite expensive. Don't let the price prevent you from purchasing the best shoe for your foot. Anything that can help lower your risk of injury from running is a valuable investment. Less expensive training shoes are only for people who have a relatively low body weight, a normal arch, and normal pronation. If you do not fall into this ideal category, spend the money for the features that will protect you.

Racing. During your regular training runs, speed is not your greatest concern. Getting fit and staying healthy is more important. But when it

Figure 2.23 Training shoes.

comes to racing, you may want to see how fast you can go. One of the things you can do to improve speed is to wear a lighter shoe. Racing shoes are lighter than training shoes, so if you wear racers you will see a slight improvement in speed (see Figure 2.24). Note, though, that the difference is just a second or two a mile faster—not really that much. Racing shoes do not provide as much cushioning and support as training shoes. Remember that in a triathlon you are already fatigued from the swim and the bike ride by the time you start running (this is a point that we'll make many times in this book). As a result, the weight you saved by wearing a racing shoe may not outweigh the comfort and protection the training shoe offers. So, before convincing yourself that you want a pair of racing shoes, think about whether you want to sacrifice the extra comfort and protection for a slight gain in speed. Athletes who are thin with normal arches and normal pronation benefit the most from wearing racing shoes.

Figure 2.24   Racing shoes.

Socks

You've got plenty of socks in your drawer already, so why buy more? Athletic socks are cushioned to protect your feet. Cycling socks are thinner than running socks, so do not use them for long runs. Running socks work fine on the bike, but be careful—you may have selected your bike shoes while wearing thin socks, and the fit will be too tight with heavier ones. If your cycling shoe feels too tight with a running sock, buy cycling socks.

Shorts

Running shorts are light and comfortable and are usually inexpensive. More expensive shorts are made from materials that keep you drier.

Tops

A singlet (see Figure 2.25) is a tank top made of a lightweight material. Designed to keep you cool, singlets are a good addition to your running wardrobe. A T-shirt also works fine, except on the hottest days.

Figure 2.25 Running singlet.

Hats

Though this is an optional item for many athletes, if you live in a very warm climate you'll need to wear a hat for your protection. The sun beating intensely down on your head can be dangerous. An exposed head in extreme heat can precipitate heat prostration or heat exhaustion.

Sunglasses

Protecting your eyes is very important. It's necessary that you wear sunglasses with ultraviolet (UV) protection (see Figure 2.26). Also the

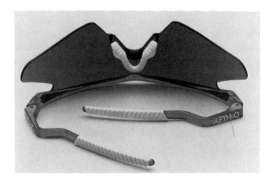

Figure 2.26 Sunglasses.

impact-resistance rating of the lenses (an ANSI rating) is important. If you wear no eye protection or a cheap pair of sunglasses, a rock kicked up by the bike tires or a passing vehicle or a crash can cause considerable damage to your eyes.

What's It Worth to You?

If you look at Table 2.6, you can see that the basic start-up costs for triathlon training add up to about $1,000. This figure drops down to $200 if you already have cycling equipment. Cycling clearly represents the majority of the cost of triathlon training.

Table 2.6
Basic Triathlon Costs

Swim and Run		Bike	
Swimsuit	$30	Road bike	$500
Goggles	25	Shoes	105
Running shoes	85	Shorts	50
Shorts	20	Jersey	65
Singlet	15	Helmet	80
		Parts	60
Subtotal:	$175	*Subtotal:*	$860
Total:	**$1,035**		

After looking at the start-up costs, you may think that triathlon training is just too expensive for you. But don't be dismayed! You can devise some cheaper ways to approach your triathlon needs. First, talk to your friends—they may have equipment that you can use. Someone may have two of something or would welcome the chance to sell an item in order to go out and buy the latest technological advancement. Second, look for used equipment. It's a good idea to take along a friend who knows about the item in question. Before making any purchase, ask if you can test the item. This applies especially to bikes: Ride a used bike before buying it to see if it suits you.

Don't try to buy every item you run across. The costs are going to add up in a hurry. If you spend your life's savings to participate in this new endeavor you'll put a lot of pressure on yourself to perform and probably won't be able to enjoy the atmosphere of triathlons. Approaching the sport with moderation, however, will enable you to participate with a good perspective.

Part II

Biomechanics

Nothing will dictate your degree of success in triathlons more than your biomechanics. Poor biomechanics leads to an unnecessary expenditure of energy and can result in continual injury. The following three chapters contain information on building a foundation on which to practice perfect biomechanics.

Chapter 3 discusses the biomechanics of swimming, the most technical of the three triathlon sports and the first event in most contests. Read these pages carefully, especially if you have not swum before; they take the mystery out of moving through the water.

Chapter 4 discusses bicycling biomechanics. As we hope you learned in chapter 2, cycling fast entails more than stomping on the pedals. Bicycling for speed is also drastically different than cruising for pleasure. Chapter 4 will give you the confidence to make your bike go fast.

Chapter 5 is more than a discussion on running biomechanics; it is a specific examination of running in a triathlon. What makes triathlon running unique is that you are already tired by the time you begin the running segment, and that complicates your biomechanics. We'll tell you how to overcome this obstacle.

Chapter 3

Swimming

Swimming presents the greatest set of challenges in the triathlon. Some people perceive learning to swim as life threatening. For them, swimming means survival, not performance. Many triathletes train for the swim phase with the simple goal of merely finishing, not competing.

Another problem with the swim is the environment. Instead of applying force against a solid surface such as in running, you now push (actually pull, then push) against a fluid medium, which offers less resistance. You need to move your body through this fluid rather than through air. Because water is 1,000 times denser than air, any slight flaw in form is magnified tremendously in the water. Because of these factors stemming from moving in a fluid environment, swimming is the least efficient of all sports.

This chapter will focus on the mechanics of the front crawl as it relates to the triathlete. The rules of the sport allow you to use any swim stroke you wish, but the most efficient stroke for triathletes is the front crawl with several modifications to breathing and sighting required in open water. The basic objectives of swim technique are (a) to minimize drag through the water, a concept called vessel shaping; and (b) to develop proper hand movement through the water, called propulsion. Ultimately, these two concepts work in harmony to contribute to the swimmer's overall speed and efficiency.

Traditionally, most instruction methods emphasize the propulsion effort. We think that you should start instead by trying to align your body properly to create a streamlined shape in relation to the water. Then you can begin to add propulsion, which results in a movement that is rhythmically powerful. You cannot paste power onto a nonrhythmic body and expect to have a great deal of success.

Triathletes are often anxious to get out and train without paying much attention to proper technique. But developing proper technique is actually more important than the time you spend logging swimming yards. Figure 3.1 speaks to the problem of swim efficiency among triathletes.

The relationship between work output and swim speed differs drastically between triathletes and competitive swimmers. Based on Figure 3.1, a triathlete working very hard in the water, say at 4 L of oxygen uptake, swims at about .8 m/sec. At 4 L output a competitive swimmer, however, swims at 1.2 m/sec. Therefore, given the same amount of work, the trained

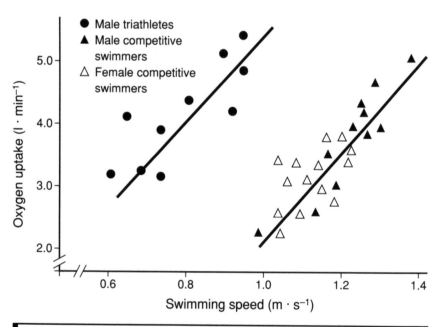

Figure 3.1 Oxygen uptake of male triathletes and competitive swimmers.

swimmer goes 50% faster. Training properly in the water will make you a very conditioned swimmer, but not necessarily an efficient or fast one. Only by training using proper technique will you be able to swim faster. It becomes very apparent that triathletes need to spend more time and effort on swim technique than on merely completing a certain number of training yards.

Experts point out that all swimmers spend at least 30% of their physical efforts correcting errors in form. Swimmers need to spend their time developing correct form, rhythm, and balance so they can begin to use their hands and feet for forward motion.

Vessel Shaping

Efficient swimmers appear to "knife" through the water with little effort. Like human torpedoes, they streamline themselves to become as small as possible in the direction they intend to move. Although swimmers have understood the importance of this concept for a long time, swim coach Bill Boomer at the University of Rochester in New York has spent considerable time articulating it. Boomer coined the term *vessel shaping*, which means attempting to minimize the space the body takes up in the water as well as the shape the body presents to the water.

Boomer is convinced that 70% of successful swimming depends on body positioning in the water and just 30% depends on hand movement—the power component. If he is correct, most triathletes have their priorities reversed and need to completely reevaluate how they spend their time in swim training.

In the water, you need to disturb as little water around you as possible. Do this by creating only those movements that are essential to the swim stroke and picturing yourself making the smallest hole possible as you cut through the water. Movements that involve excessive body roll, head bobbing, a large kick, and even a high arm recovery work against this principle.

In general, a long, narrow body can swim faster because it creates less drag on the water. Keeping your head, arms, and legs moving in an imaginary straight line is the goal. When you rotate your body from side to side, rotate around this same straight line.

In addition to presenting a streamlined body shape to the water, you must think about your body position as you move through the water. Even if you make yourself very small, if you are not horizontal with the water, as shown in Figure 3.2, you will create excessive drag. Swimmers who

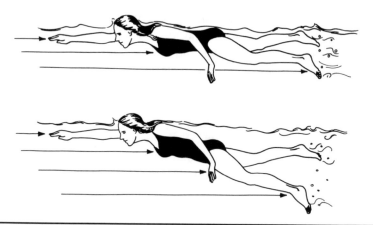

Figure 3.2 Horizontal alignment and the added resistance when the body is not horizontal to the water.

wriggle from side to side (lateral alignment) can also create inefficiency. With vessel shaping you combine these two concepts, enabling you not only to become streamlined in the water but also to maintain streamlined shape horizontally with minimal side-to-side action.

To improve your horizontal alignment (best viewed from the side), make every effort to keep your body as parallel to the surface of the water as possible. The water line should be approximately at your hairline; keep your eyes focused forward and a little down. Even when you roll to one side to take a breath, maintain this linear position. Poor horizontal alignment can occur from kicking too deep. Remember, you should kick only slightly lower than an imaginary line extending back from the deepest part of your trunk.

Figure 3.3 illustrates good lateral alignment (a view from above) and excessive left/right movement of the hips and legs away from the upper body. Swimmers with poor lateral alignment tend to snake through the water. Generally, they cause this problem by overreaching when the hand enters the water. It can also be the result of lifting the head during breathing.

Just as in vessel shaping, you use horizontal and lateral alignment together to make the smallest hole possible in the water. The biggest problem in maintaining good horizontal and lateral alignment come from your need to remain small but also to ''roll'' at the shoulders with each arm pull. This body roll is necessary for three things: First, dropping your shoulder puts your arm in the best position to pull against the water. Second, this roll allows your recovery arm to clear the water easily. Third, body roll is important for breathing. When done properly, body roll is greatest at the shoulders, yet very minimal at the head and hips. Viewed from the front, body roll should entail about a 45-degree turn to each side, as shown in Figure 3.4.

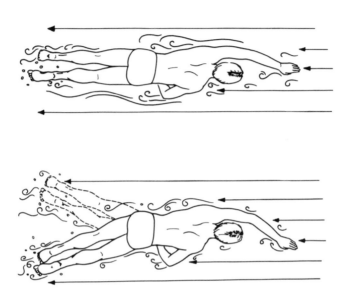

Figure 3.3 Lateral alignment and the effect of excessive side-to-side body movements on drag in the front crawl stroke.

Figure 3.4 The body roll as seen from the front.

Creating Movement or Propulsion

In rowing, force is applied through a paddle that is basically flat with a large surface area that contacts the water. In a motorboat, force is applied through a turning propeller, pitched at such an angle that it pulls water to it, then pushes this same water away. The faster the spin and the bigger the propeller, the faster the boat goes. Current swim technology suggests that the swimmer's hand creates both types of force. It pulls back like a paddle and also angles on an out-in path to effect a propeller-type force.

Think about sticking your hand out a car window while cruising down the highway. When the leading edge of the hand pitches up slightly, the hand rises. In swimming, you apply the same principle by slightly opening the leading edge of your hand in the direction of the outward or inward path. But be careful to angle minimally. The more you angle your hand, the less effective the paddle component of the movement will be. The combined movement makes an S shape, as shown in Figure 3.5.

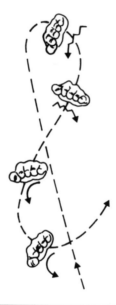

Figure 3.5   Proper hand patterns for the front crawl.

The Arm Stroke

The arm stroke in the front crawl is broken down into six phases—entry, downsweep, catch, insweep, upsweep, and recovery. Each arm goes through this cycle in about a second.

Entry Phase.   Entry is the point at which your hand and arm enter the water. This point should be forward of the head and about 8 to 10 in. short of full extension, as shown in Figure 3.6. Entry is slightly to the side of the body's midline with the palm facing out. The thumb side of the hand should enter the water first. Once your hand enters the water, you should attempt to move the wrist, elbow, and shoulder through the

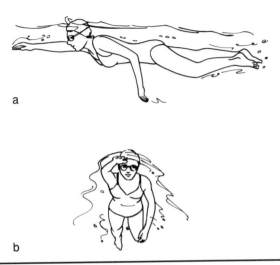

Figure 3.6 Right arm position at the entry phase and the left arm position at the beginning of the upsweep phase, side (a) and front (b).

same hole that your hand cut in the water. At the completion of the entry, the arm should be extended fully, with the elbow locked out.

Downsweep Phase. Here you should sweep down and out in a curvilinear path. The downward direction engages the paddle motion, and the outward movement simulates the propeller movement. Swim coaches describe the position of the downsweep as if your arm were wrapped around the curved portion of a barrel. Avoid dropping your elbow during the downsweep. The elbow should remain above the rest of the forearm. The purpose of the downsweep is not to generate great amounts of power, but merely to get your arm in position for the remaining power phases and to position your hand for the catch phase.

Catch Phase. Once your arm is properly positioned near the end of the downsweep, flex your wrist down and out. At this point you should be able to feel a solid handful of water. Keep your fingers together (or only slightly apart), not allowing water to slip through (see Figure 3.7).

Insweep Phase. The three previous phases prepare you for the insweep, the first of the two power phases. The insweep begins at the deepest point of the downsweep. Your hand begins with an in-and-back path. The insweep starts outside and below the shoulder and finishes close to the center of the body (see Figure 3.8). Notice that the hand changes pitch as it moves through the center portion of the S sweep. As the hand begins to travel toward the center of the body, the elbow flexes to allow the

Figure 3.7   Arm position at the beginning of the catch phase, side (a) and front (b).

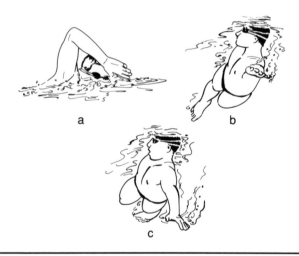

Figure 3.8   The right arm position at the beginning of the insweep phase (a), the mid-insweep position of the left arm (b), and the end position of the insweep phase of the left arm (c).

hand to rise up and closer to the body. During this phase, the hand accelerates somewhat in preparation for the fast upsweep phase.

The greatest difficulty in executing a proper insweep appears to be the pitch of the hand as it moves in, up, and back. When you fail to change the pitch as the directions change, your hand tends to slip through the water without creating any propulsive force.

Upsweep Phase.   The upsweep phase is a powerful push, first backward from the chest to the waist, and then up, out, and back until the elbow approaches full extension (see Figure 3.9). Coaches suggest that if you do it properly, you should feel your thumb brush the outside of your thigh. When your hand approaches your thigh, the propulsive upsweep force is complete. Your hand should then rotate inward to release the pressure on the water and edge out with minimal drag. The upsweep is the most powerful phase of the stroke, but many swimmers miss this benefit by pulling the hand out of the water at the waist, short of midthigh.

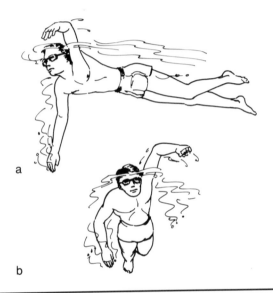

Figure 3.9   Right arm position at the beginning (a) and the end (b) of the upsweep phase.

Recovery Phase.   Although the arm recovery does not contribute to the propulsion force, if poorly executed, it can result in compromised efficiency, timing, and body alignment. Your objective in the recovery phase is to reposition your arm for another stroke. The preferred technique uses a high-elbow recovery because it is more efficient and does not disturb body alignment.

Recovery begins where the upsweep ends. The elbow breaks through the water while the hand is completing the upsweep. The elbow moves forward and up while slightly flexed. As the shoulder rotates, the bend in the elbow becomes greater, causing the hand to follow close to the water's surface. The hand continues to move forward until it is repositioned to once again begin the entry phase of the stroke. Remember that the recovery is not a forced effort but is smooth and relaxed. Keeping your muscles tense during the recovery phase will restrict valuable blood flow and ultimately lead to premature fatigue.

If the timing between the arms is correct, one of your arms will always be providing propulsive force: While one arm completes the entry and begins the downsweep and catch, the other is finishing the upsweep.

The Flutter Kick

The flutter kick is important for stabilizing the arm stroke and can help you maintain horizontal alignment by keeping your waist area up on the water's surface. But don't depend on the flutter kick to power you forward. In fact, the flutter kick resists forward motion when the arms are working effectively. In addition, researchers have observed that the flutter kick requires four times the energy the arms need to cover the same distance. Therefore, triathletes need to conserve their kicking effort, expending only enough energy to stabilize the trunk and possibly aid in keeping the body horizontal to the water's surface.

We can break down the flutter kick into two distinct movements: the downbeat and the upbeat. Picture your lower leg as if it were loosely attached; your thigh tends to lead the lower leg throughout its entire movement. The lower leg continues to sweep downward with the knee flexed 30 to 40 degrees and the toes pointed as much as possible. At the end of the downbeat, the foot should be 12 to 14 in. deep but only slightly deeper than your chest.

In the upbeat portion of the kick, your hip and knee once again lead the movement, so that even before the foot completes the downward segment, the hip and knee are beginning the upbeat phase. The feet are still pointed from the ankle but not forcefully so. The flutter kick movement is shown in Figure 3.10.

In coordinating the proper timing of your arm and leg movements, first determine the number of kicks you execute in each stroke cycle. Variations appear to consist of either two, four, or six beats for each complete stroke cycle (two arm strokes). When you critically need to conserve energy, the two-beat kick will be your best choice; however, when optimal speed is the issue, such as in a sprint swim, then the four- and six-beat kicks are appropriate.

Breathing

Coordinating all the movements discussed previously into one fluid motion is difficult enough. Now you must add the important function of breathing.

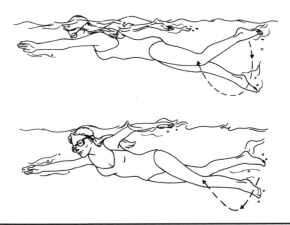

Figure 3.10 Leg movements of the flutter kick.

You should incorporate turning your head sideways to breathe into your body roll. When you have rolled maximally toward your breathing side, expose your mouth to the air temporarily without exaggerating the body roll at all and with only a minimal additional roll of your head. Begin turning your head when the arm opposite your breathing side enters the water. This allows your head roll to precede the body roll and gives you extra time to expose your mouth above water to take your breath.

You must turn your head with much of your head remaining in the water. Because the head weighs about 16 pounds, lifting it out of the water forces the rest of your body, especially the trunk area, deeper into the water. Horizontal alignment is sacrificed, resulting in added drag.

You should also coordinate returning your face to the water with your body roll. Practice exhaling while your face is underwater, but don't exhale completely. If you should find a wave instead of air when you go to take your next breath, you'll be glad you saved some of that last air. Maintaining a small air reserve also aids in buoyancy.

Proper swim technique is a complex integration of body positioning, breathing, and arm power. We have broken down the front crawl into these and other components. Obviously, they must be cooperatively integrated to function as a single unit. As a practical way of determining your overall effectiveness in the front crawl movement, count the number of arm strokes you require to swim 25 yards. Competitive distance swimmers take about 13 to 15 strokes; triathletes should work on their technique until they can consistently take about 20 strokes (10 complete cycles) for 25 yards. Don't concentrate on training distances until you attain this goal. Remember, practice makes permanent, not perfect. So when you begin to need more than 20 strokes to swim 25 yards, return to practicing proper technique.

Tips for a Better Performance

A swimmer's need for oxygen is directly related to his or her swimming efficiency. Poor swimmers face a kind of double jeopardy—their greater oxygen demands create a hurried or short-reaching stroke. Also, the sensation of always needing a deep breath of air can cause the triathlete tremendous anxiety.

A swimming pool, with its buoys, lifeguards, and nearby decks, is a fine place to practice your stroke technique; because you know that help is near, fear is minimized. But when you find yourself practicing in open water without all that security, anxiety can gnaw away at your self-confidence.

Begin open-water training when the water is relatively calm and warm enough to minimize any fear of hypothermia. It is also helpful to seek out a stretch of water shallow enough so that you can stand up if panic should strike. If you cannot find shallow water, have a friend escort you in a boat or on a surfboard.

Your initial experiences with open-water swimming will orient you to the motionless sensation you experience when you can no longer see the bottom passing beneath you. For some, this can be frightening. In a race, if you cannot see yourself moving through the water, you must logically realize that if you are performing the stroke as you usually do, then you must be making forward progress.

Swim training in a pool can also give you a false sense of confidence in your ability to swim straight. Just because you don't collide with the lane buoys during your pool workout doesn't mean you'll be able to swim straight in open water. In fact, it's conceivable that you might swim in complete circles in open water if you never were to sight for direction. Even highly skilled swimmers can find themselves off course because of currents and waves. All open-water swimmers must respect the need to sight for direction. Sighting is orienting yourself toward fixed landmarks, regularly checking your orientation so that you will move directly to an intended point.

In your early experiences with open-water swimming, you might practice sighting off your floating escort, but sooner or later you must confront the problem of sighting forward and to the side. If you can clearly see landmarks while in the water, you can sight by *peeking*. The technique is as follows: Just before you normally return your face to the water after inhaling, turn your head forward, quickly locate your point of reference, and then submerge your face. Once back into your normal stroke, correct your direction by pulling wider with the arm that is opposite the direction you intend to go. This will reorient your lateral alignment without requiring you to stop, shift, and begin forward motion all over again.

To get your bearings if the water is particularly rough or the reference points are small, you may have to incorporate a water polo stroke, which is doing the front crawl with your head out of the water for the entire stroke cycle. Because this movement requires an accentuated kick, your initial experiences with this technique can be exhausting. Practice this technique thoroughly before competing in open water. Most open-water swimmers will sight every five to eight stroke cycles.

Bilateral Breathing

Distance swimmers often recommend using a bilateral breathing technique (breathing on both sides), which they claim helps to "round out" your stroke. In the triathlon swim, learning to breathe on both sides allows you to sight to the side regardless of the course design. The buoys that direct your swim route can be on either side of you as you swim, so if you can bilateral breathe, you can orient yourself with the buoys regardless of whether they're on your left or right side.

The bilateral technique is a system whereby you breathe once every cycle and a half instead of once every cycle. Bilateral breathing teaches you to roll your body equally to both sides, causing you to develop equal pulling strength in both arms. This balancing benefit enables you to swim in a straighter line.

Although these benefits are attractive, this technique does compromise the quantity of oxygen made available to the lungs. Bilateral breathers take one fewer breath every three stroke cycles than swimmers who practice conventional breathing. This decrease in oxygen availability can result in premature fatigue as well as the anxiety associated with being in an oxygen deficit.

To counter these problems, learn to bilateral breathe without the frequent change of breathing sides. After breathing about five stroke cycles on one side, switch to the other side by delaying your breath an additional half stroke, and remain on the other side for about five stroke cycles. Make sure you are very comfortable with bilateral breathing before attempting this technique in open water.

Drafting

Another technique to improve your swimming in competition is to *draft* off another swimmer. The technique is perfectly legal and can decrease your work output by as much as 30%! This is the same principle used in biking—namely, you stay close to and in the same path as the swimmer ahead of you. Be careful not to disturb the kick of the swimmer you're drafting off of. He or she might just slow slightly and give you a swift kick in the head.

Finally, learn to accept distractions while swimming. Many swimmers train in water that is calm, clear, peaceful, and free of obstructions. On race day, bodies are constantly encroaching your domain, and other swimmers' arms and feet are getting tangled up in your stroke. Realize, however, that your competitors aren't attempting to complicate your stroke. They are merely trying to survive and negotiate through the same problems that you are.

Wet Suits

In chapter 2 we discussed the various designs of wet suits and when to use them. Triathlons encourage athletes to wear wet suits to protect against hypothermia during swimming. But another definite benefit to wearing a wet suit is its ability to keep you buoyant. We did a small, simple study to test this point. We underwater weighed a swimmer wearing a swimsuit, neoprene knickers, a long john–style wet suit, and a full, long-sleeved wet suit. The swimmer's effective buoyancy wearing these different suits is shown in Table 3.1. Next, we counted how many strokes it took the swimmer to swim 25 yards wearing the different suits. As you can see in Table 3.1, the differences were dramatic. We also filmed the swimmer underwater, and the horizontal alignment was tremendously improved. Based on these observations, we must conclude that wet suits offer a definite competitive advantage.

Table 3.1
Wet Suit Study

Design	Buoyancy (g)	% Fat (Theoretical)	Strokes/25 yd
Swimsuit	0	5%	27
Knickers	1,875	17.9%	24
Long john	3,150	26%	22
Full wet suit	4,720	37.1%	20

In this chapter we introduced many new concepts that run counter to traditional swim training. Instead of emphasizing swimming long distances, we believe that swim training needs to focus more on proper swim technique. By technique, we mean vessel shaping, not arm movement through the water. The triathlete will see measurable improvement only after he or she improves body position in the water. Water is too viscous to tolerate technique errors, and adding power to an inefficient stroke only magnifies those errors.

Because it is impossible to see your own vessel shape in the water, feedback from a coach, a fellow swimmer, or videotape analysis becomes critical. You may think your technique is perfect, but until you can see it for yourself, you will continue to practice those errors and eventually make them permanent. Incorporate into your training the stroke drills that follow. They allow you to focus on one single part of your stroke and require you to practice a more perfect technique.

Swimming Drills

Swimming stroke drills let you focus on and refine one particular phase of the swim stroke.

Front Crawl Breathing

It is imperative to keep the head–spine alignment intact when you breathe. Practice this by breathing when you look to the 10 o'clock position on the left side and the 2 o'clock position on the right side. This will point your head out and up with the rest of the body remaining straight.

Head Up

Keeping the head up increases sensitivity to the catch position and enhances leverage on the water during the first third of the stroke pull. To train, practice swimming water-polo style, with your chin at the surface of the water and your eyes straight ahead while you stroke.

Drag Fingertip

During the recovery phase of the stroke, bend your elbows and purposely drag your fingertips across the water's surface. This drill helps you focus on keeping the hand low during recovery.

Fist Swimming

Swim with your hands in a fist to force your forearm to maintain proper positioning perpendicular to the direction of pull.

Single Arm Crawl "A"

To enhance the feel of proper positioning of the hand in the water, practice the single arm crawl. This helps eliminate favoring one arm's effectiveness over the other. To practice, take the stroking arm through proper motion while the other arm simply remains extended in front. Switch stroking arms each pool length.

Single Arm Crawl "B"

To determine the effectiveness of the final upsweep phase, use this variation of the single arm crawl. Take the stroking arm through proper movement while the other arm is trailing alongside the body. Switch arms each length. If done correctly, you will feel an extra thrust at the end of the stroke, and you will not experience excessive body roll.

Catch-Up

To emphasize the importance of a long arm stroke and enhance the sensitivity to the catch phase and body rotation following the outsweep, practice this drill. Extend both arms in front and take a stroke. As you complete the stroke cycle, bring the stroking hand together with the stationary hand. Then stroke again, this time with the other hand. For each stroke, the other arm does not begin until the first one has completed the pull and recovery and your hands have made contact.

Front Crawl Speed

Using proper technique, attempt to increase the tempo at which you stroke in the front crawl (which increases your swimming speed). Focus on a rapid, correct pull through the water. Swim short distances, starting out with a slower stroke cadence and gradually increasing to your maximum speed.

Hip Rotation

To maximize the time you are on your side during the front crawl (the position that creates least drag), practice doing as quickly as you can the rotation of your hips, going from one side during arm recovery to the other during the catch phase.

Chapter 4

Cycling

When we consider all means of travel powered by physical effort, bicycling emerges as the quickest and most efficient. Cyclists with special equipment, refined skill, and lots of stamina frequently post speeds of more than 100 mph while drafting behind motorized vehicles.

Whether speed, efficiency, or simply chance brought bicycling into the triathlon, it provides the sharpest possible contrast to swimming in terms of physical performance. Swimming lacks speed and requires only minimal equipment; cycling incorporates both to a great degree. Cycling is short on biomechanics; swimming requires a refined technique.

In this chapter we'll investigate cycling training techniques designed specifically for triathlon competition.

After you've been properly outfitted with your ideal triathlon bike, you should focus your efforts on cycling techniques. Resist the constant temptation to upgrade your bike in an effort to achieve a minuscule advantage over the competition. Knowledge of proper cycling mechanics applied in a concentrated strategic manner is the way to achieve successful cycling performance. Don't be surprised to find yourself pedaling alone in this effort. Few individuals are willing to invest the time and concentrated hard work needed to improve their cycling skills. Unfortunately, it's all too easy to be a "bike techie"—to use all the cycling jargon, to have all the latest equipment, and to know all the big names in the sport. But when it comes time to perform, techies are still developing their basic training program.

In keeping with the principle that practice makes permanent, you must ingrain the proper cycling mechanics into your mind and be ready to apply them to all your workouts. Cyclists who lack this prerequisite understanding will eventually perfect their mistakes to the point where progress ceases or injury occurs.

Pedaling Efficiency

Developing pedaling efficiency is probably the cyclist's greatest concern. Because of this, triathletes and cyclists want to perfect the techniques of pedaling mechanics and pedal cadence. Traditionally, the goal in pedaling mechanics was to develop smooth circular strokes, applying fairly even pressure throughout a large part of the stroke circle. This has been called *spinning*, and most people thought it was something good cyclists do. Everybody wanted to be able to spin, but it did not come easily.

Exercise physiologists have demonstrated more recently that elite cyclists are better not because they can spin, but because they produce, in the physiologists' words, "larger propulsive torques by creating significantly larger forces pushing down on the pedal than at any other point in the vertical direction on the pedal during the downstroke and not by attempting to pull up on the pedal during the upstroke."

What this means, and as you can see in Figure 4.1, is that the cyclist's mean torque (rotational force) production is greatest at about 90 degrees. More torque means more force, and that means going faster. Ninety degrees equates to the 3 o'clock position of the cycling stroke. So when your foot is in the 3 o'clock position you can create more force than at any other point.

Figure 4.2 shows another way to represent the forces produced during the cycling stroke. The longest arrow, representing the greatest force, is at 3 o'clock. Note that some force is still produced at 7, 8, and 9 o'clock. For this force to be useful to the cyclist, though, the arrows would have to point up! Do not be alarmed by this; you create tremendous force on the downstroke, and inertia alone will require some time to slow this downward force. The force does not immediately change direction.

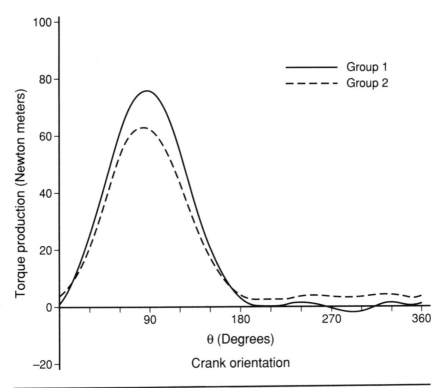

Figure 4.1 Average torque production at varying degrees of crank orientation in two groups when cycling at the average power output maintained for 1 hour.

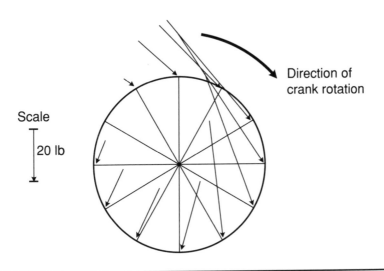

Figure 4.2 Direction and intensity of forces being applied to the pedals when proper pedal mechanics are in effect.

Experts used to think that in spinning the cyclist spread the forces evenly over the entire stroke circle. But if a cyclist applied fairly even pressure throughout a large part of the stroke circle, the lines in Figure 4.1 would be nearly horizontal. There would be no peak, just a straight line. So it is obvious, then, that the best cyclists do not spin after all.

Another technique that cyclists thought they had to practice was *ankling*. This was a distinct and deliberate movement—flexing and extending the ankle. Recent studies, however, have shown that the term ankling is somewhat of a misnomer. For greatest efficiency, the pedal stroke should follow the natural motion of the foot (see Figure 4.3). Exaggerating the foot motion creates premature fatigue because it shortens the foot's rest phase. Because blood flows through a muscle only when it is not con-

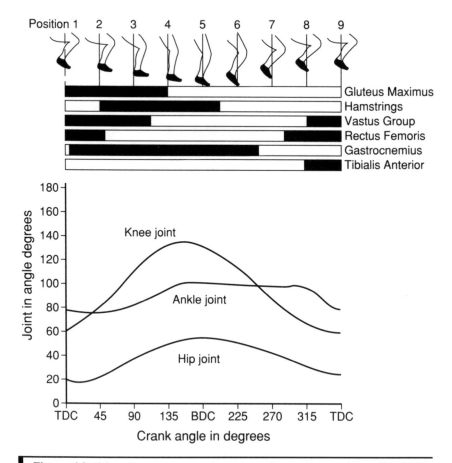

Figure 4.3 Movement patterns and corresponding muscle activity of a highly skilled cyclist.

tracting, oxygen and other vital nutrients are limited, resulting in high levels of lactic acid and fatigue.

Pedal pressure applied in a pistonlike manner utilizes primarily the powerful hip extensor muscle group called the gluteal muscles, with the gluteus maximus doing most of the work. The muscles that create knee flexion and extension contribute little to this movement; the knee merely serves as a hinge allowing the cyclist to complete the circular pedal motion. Although pedaling in smooth, even-pressured circles helps the gluteal muscles by incorporating some knee extension and knee flexion during appropriate phases of the entire circular pedal motion, this does not produce much torque. Maximum torque occurs at the same position in the stroke, whether you pedal in an up-and-down pistonlike motion or in a circular motion. The majority of your torque occurs in the 12 o'clock to 6 o'clock positions. As mentioned already, you achieve maximum torque at approximately 90 degrees or 3 o'clock (see Figure 4.1). You begin to lose power after the forward horizontal position, or approximately 4 o'clock. After the 6 o'clock position, little torque is produced. The piston-type pedaler works mostly in the 12 o'clock to 6 o'clock area, using mainly the gluteal muscles and letting momentum move the pedals into proper position for the opposite hip to take action. If you find yourself shifting back and forth on your seat with each pedal rotation, you are not applying force in a vertical fashion.

Preceding the action of the hip extensors is the force applied by the knee extensor muscle group called the quadriceps, or quads. As shown in Figure 4.4a, the quadriceps begin applying force to the knee in a forward horizontal direction at approximately 11 o'clock. Once the pedal is in the forward quadrant, the gluteal muscles contribute to the movement, allowing for torque to be applied in both a forward and a downward direction (see Figure 4.4b). After the crank arm reaches the forward horizontal position, the quads no longer contribute to the movement be- cause the pedal is ultimately forward at this point. A pull to the rear complements the downward force still being applied by the hip extensors. You create this added torque by contracting the knee flexors, a muscle group located in the posterior thigh collectively called the hamstrings. Figure 4.4c shows that the hamstrings begin a pull on the crank arms to the rear from approximately 4 o'clock to 7 o'clock. During most of the phase when the hamstrings are working, the gluteals are resting, because the downward torque loses its effectiveness somewhere around 4 to 5 o'clock.

In effect, three distinct muscle groups are involved in proper pedaling mechanics: the quads initiate the movement at the 11 o'clock position;

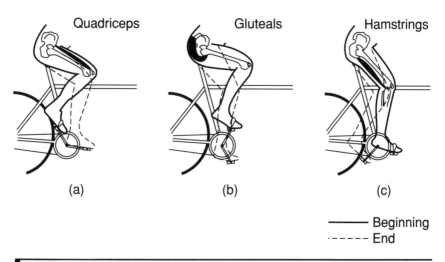

Quadriceps   Gluteals   Hamstrings

(a)   (b)   (c)

———— Beginning
----- End

Figure 4.4   Coordination of the three major muscle groups used in proper pedaling mechanics.

the gluteals complement the work at approximately the 1 o'clock position; the work of the quads is complete at approximately 3 o'clock; and the hamstrings take over and complete the stroke at around the 7 or 8 o'clock position. As contraction of the hamstrings tapers off, the quads begin contracting again.

To avoid confusion, let's make a clarification. The stroke mechanics of a sprint cyclist are different from those of an endurance-oriented cyclist. A cyclist who sprints utilizes more muscle groups: muscles that move the ankle and more of the thigh muscles. Another difference is that instead of beginning the pedal force at 11 o'clock and concluding at 8 o'clock, the sprint cyclist eliminates the rest phase between 8 and 11 o'clock because the hamstrings contract throughout most of the circle. In addition, one of the quadriceps muscles (rectus femoris) is capable of hip flexion and therefore contracts between 7 o'clock and 12 o'clock. This helps pull the pedal up until it is in position for all the quads to begin extending the knee.

The ultimate objective in sprinting is speed with little regard for efficiency. Considering the relatively short distance involved in a typical time trial or criterium race (approximately 25 mi), the trained cyclist can afford to expend tremendous amounts of energy and generate relatively high levels of lactic acid. But for the triathlete, this would result in a poor running performance after completion of the bike segment.

Triathletes need to be concerned with optimal performance in the context of efficiency. By pedaling with powerful downward movements and utilizing the hip extensors and both sets of thigh muscles, cyclists can be assured that their training will progress optimally.

Pedal Cadence

After developing the proper pedaling movement, you'll want to combine it with the proper pedal cadence. Pedal cadence refers to the number of revolutions completed per minute (rpm). For the touring cyclist, pedal cadence is somewhere between 60 and 80 rpm. Competitive cyclists seldom fall below a 90-rpm cadence and can usually pedal effectively at as high as 120 rpm. The energy-conscious triathlete will probably range between 70 and 90 rpm and more realistically between 80 and 90 rpm.

As we mentioned earlier, blood flows through muscles only when they are relaxed. But muscles in contraction can also aid in blood flow because blood is squeezed forward when the muscle is contracted. The trick in cycling, then, is to create a contraction and relaxation rate that will allow optimal blood flow through the muscle. Slow pedal cadences stop blood flow momentarily because the contractile phase is too long. High cadences, on the other hand, use many additional muscle groups in trying to stabilize the joints that are being radically thrashed around. Settle on a cadence that is comfortable for you, but try to maintain a rate somewhere between 70 and 90 rpm. As you become more skilled and efficient, you will undoubtedly work longer at cadences closer to 90 than to 70 rpm.

The easiest way to check cadence is with a cyclecomputer equipped with a cadence function (see p. 30). If you do not have a cyclecomputer that monitors cadence, then try the following. First, you'll need a watch capable of displaying seconds. Next, head out for a flat road. After you are thoroughly warmed up, count the number of complete revolutions you pedal in a minute. Although this is not exact, it is an approximate reference to make sure you are cycling at cadences faster than one revolution per second but no faster than three revolutions every 2 sec.

Gearing

Once you have settled on an ideal cadence, you should try to maintain that rate throughout your entire workout, with the possible exception of when you're on hills. To do so, you will need to carefully select proper gearing based on your abilities and the terrain you will be confronting. Proper gearing allows you to put forth approximately the same amount of effort at all times. The gearing on most low to moderately priced bikes is totally unacceptable for this objective. Those bikes provide a massive range between the smallest and the largest cogs on the freewheel.

The gears associated with the cranks and pedals are called *chain rings*. The smaller gear has between 39 and 42 teeth; the larger gear has either 52 or 53 teeth.

The gears associated with the rear wheel are called the *freewheel* or *rear cluster*. They generally range between 12 and 28 teeth. Whether you have 5, 6, 7, or even 8 gears in your rear cluster, you can write out the gearing using numbers separated by dashes. For example, 12-14-16-18-20-22 means a six-gear freewheel; the smallest gear has 12 teeth and the largest has 22 teeth.

Wide ranges leave big gaps between gears; consequently, riders may find themselves spinning frantically in one gear and then having to strain their muscles in the next. A technique you may find effective is to have the gears very close together in the range where you do most of your riding, but spread the last two gears in the rear cog out farther to help you climb the hills.

Because rear clusters are cheap and easy to change, carry several along and decide which gear range to use after you review the course. When training in relatively flat areas, you can use a rear cluster with a 13-14-15-17-19-21 arrangement on a 52- and 42-tooth front chain ring. An example of typical gearing and cadence is a 52/15 (chain ring/freewheel) gear with an 80 cadence; this will move you along at approximately 21 mph. For hilly competition, you might try using a 13-14-15-16-19-24 rear cluster, which will get you up steep hills but still allows you close gearing for the flats between hills.

A typical gearing for cyclists competing on the Hawaiian Ironman course is a seven-speed cluster of 12-13-14-15-16-20-22 (the 12 through 16 go up one tooth per gear, and are referred to as "single-step"), not so much for the sake of the hills but because of the tremendous head- and tailwinds. The course also presents several long downhill opportunities where you can gain on your competitors if you don't run out of gears. This is when having a 12-tooth cog comes in handy, although you'll use it infrequently. The single-step cogs are helpful because when the winds are gusty and shifting, you'll want to gear up or down in small increments.

Riding Position

Another important consideration that creates more efficient movement is riding position. How you position yourself on the bike affects aerodynamics and the mechanical advantage of your leg muscles. The term mechanical advantage suggests that an optimal joint angle exists at which each muscle offers the greatest contractile force. If your seat position is correctly set, riding position will have little effect on the muscles that work the knee and ankle. The muscles likely to be most affected by riding position are the powerful hip extensors. These muscles can offer the greatest torque when you keep your upper torso in a more horizontal position. Figure 4.5 shows how the lowest wind resistance results from the full crouch

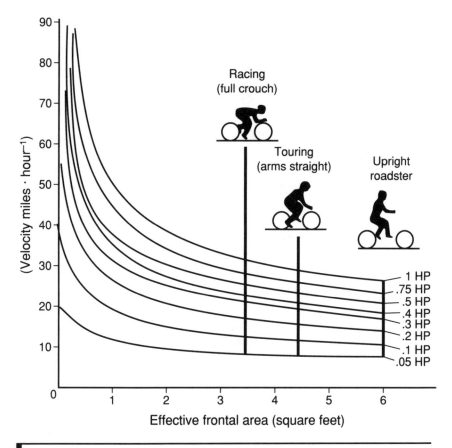

Figure 4.5   The effect of a streamlined body position is to improve the performance of human-powered vehicles at all levels of power input.

position. This position is also not very comfortable. You'll have to practice in this position before riding this way for extended periods.

You alter your riding position mainly by changing the position of your hands on the bars. Cyclists generally use two different positions, illustrated in Figure 4.6. Notice that in each position the elbows bend slightly, increasing the shock absorption lessening the stiffness of your ride. As Figure 4.6b illustrates, the regular aero position is quite aerodynamic (creating low wind resistance) and more comfortable (the hands are not under pressure). Remember this as a valuable option when you bike.

Triathletes might benefit from getting extra practice in using the hand position shown in Figure 4.6b. Consider saving position 4.6a for climbing and sprints. Riding the drops for long periods will undoubtedly give you a stiff, sore back that will decrease your performance in the run phase that follows.

The aerodynamics of cycling are somewhat complex, but they play an extremely important role in cycling efficiency when you are going faster than 10 mph. Air resistance accounts for more than 80% of the total force acting to slow the rider at speeds over 18 mph. And, as shown in Figure 4.5, the cyclist's work output increases exponentially as speeds increase. Notice also that an aerodynamic riding position offers you considerably faster speeds at the same work output. Consider the following: Riding while exerting 0.3 horsepower allows you to pedal at 22 mph in the full crouch racing position but at only 18 mph in the upright roadster position. You must evaluate the energy cost needed to pursue increases in speed. Efficiency usually takes precedence over riding comfort.

As you can see from Figure 4.5, the energy cost of cycling at 20 mph in the full crouch racing position is 0.25 horsepower—a reasonable work load for a trained cyclist. If the cyclist wishes to increase speed to 25 mph, the work output nearly doubles.

Wind resistance has a tremendous effect on the energy cost of cycling at speeds greater than 18 mph. Because of this, you must carefully evaluate whether you want to commit significantly more energy to gain a small increase in speed. Possibly a more efficient use of your limited energy stores would be to increase your running speed instead. In running, the work required to overcome wind drag is negligible, which allows your work output to go directly into movement.

Cycling up and down hills presents a new set of challenges. When pedaling uphill, you generally do best to combine a reduced gear ratio with a reduced pedal cadence. Because hills require you to use brute power, seek out a gear that you can pedal at a cadence of about 70 rpm.

a

b

Figure 4.6 Acceptable handlebar and hand positions using the aero drop position (a) and the regular aero position (b).

Two acceptable hill-climbing positions are pedaling in and out of the saddle. Figure 4.7 illustrates in-saddle climbing. The position is similar to that of normal riding, but you keep your torso more horizontal. Because power is so important in climbing hills, this lower position allows the hip extensors to exert more force. Figure 4.8 illustrates out-of-saddle climbing. This position allows you to use more of your body weight, and

Figure 4.7   Acceptable in-saddle hill-climbing position.

Figure 4.8   Acceptable out-of-saddle hill-climbing position.

it gives you the opportunity to stretch out muscles that are tired from being in the sitting position for a long time. However, maintaining this position for an extended period saps your energy.

Riding downhill can give your body a brief but much-needed rest. As soon as the grade points down, move through your gears quickly, assume an aerodynamic profile, and spin out in your highest gear. Once you have reached your top cadence, lower yourself into the bike with your elbows tucked in, the crank arms horizontal to the ground, and your knees pulled inward. See Figure 4.9 for a demonstration of this position.

Figure 4.9 Proper downhill aerodynamic positioning.

Training for the Competitor

The greatest formula for success in cycling is simply spending time in the saddle. There are other ways to maximize your effectiveness, but the bottom line is getting accustomed to riding for long periods. If you have the opportunity to train on the actual competition course, you can maximize training by attempting to match your training to the demands the actual race will require. This applies to distance as well as terrain.

A trap cyclists fall into easily is training at a level of mediocrity. You may grind out mile after mile, workout after workout, without seeing any real improvement from your efforts. Realistically, it is very difficult to produce quality miles day after day without any outside help. One of the best ways to break through training mediocrity, or what some people call "garbage miles," is to ride with a local bike-racing club during some of their distance-training sessions. Although some of the components of their training—drafting off each other, attacking hills, and mixing up their sprint segments—are not conducive to triathlon training, the change of pace is very healthy for you and can serve as an index of your true capabilities.

Successful cycle training and competition require a quality mix of physical and mental toughness. The cycling phase of the triathlon offers competitors a tremendous variety of excuses to justify dropping out. Flat tires and other mechanical problems are obvious obstacles, but equally lethal are the mental battles you'll confront when you face mile after mile of strong headwinds, rolling hills, or a combination of the two. Prepare yourself both mentally and physically for the unexpected, because you'll surely encounter it when the going gets tough.

Chapter 5

Running

Physically, running is the most demanding of the three sports in the triathlon. It is the only sport in which you must carry your total body weight. In swimming, you can float when fatigued; in biking you perform while sitting and you get an occasional rest from downhills and tailwinds. But where can you find respite while running? Even running downhill plays havoc with the body. To compound these problems even further, the triathlete usually begins the running phase in a fatigued, overheated, semidehydrated state, How, then, can you make the best of the run phase?

In this chapter, we examine proper running form and point out some of the technique problems the triathlete faces. Researchers and coaches have identified proper running form for most running events. What remains confusing, however, is how the fatigued condition and its unique set of problems affect you while running. Let's first examine the ideal situation (fresh running condition) and identify the pitfalls in the more realistic one (fatigued running condition).

Fresh-Run Mechanics

Fresh-run mechanics focuses on optimal running economy. You optimize running economy by eliminating unnecessary movement. Every runner operates at a certain percentage of "perfect" running form. Genetic ability is one of two major factors that determine how close to "perfect" a runner can perform. The other is practicing with good form. It is vital to remember that practice does not make perfect; *perfect* practice makes perfect.

In the past, running economy was considered less important. Runners paid attention instead to improving their aerobic capacity, assuming that was the only way they could compete at higher levels. Your aerobic capacity is defined by the amount of oxygen your body can utilize for fuel. According to this principle, if you increase the amount of fuel you utilize, the "engine" (your muscles) will produce more movement. That movement, however, must be in a specific form to produce an increase in speed. In running, that desired movement is linear. To use the simplest terminology, runners want all their energy to produce straight-ahead movement.

Observers later found that in some of the best distance runners aerobic capacities were high, but not extremely so. Instead, these elite runners were very economical—they wasted no energy and produced straight-ahead movement. In light of this discovery, researchers began to look at the running movement with a new perspective—that of reducing wasted motion.

Among elite distance runners, the best-known economical runners are Frank Shorter and Derek Clayton, and the least economical are Jim Ryun and Craig Virgin. Clayton describes his economical running movement:

> When I started training for marathon distances, my style changed naturally. Running 20 miles a day cut down on my stride length. It also eliminated the tendency to lift my knees. Gradually, my power stride evolved into one of economy. Despite the energy-draining action of my upper body, I developed a very natural leg action I call the "Clayton shuffle." Through miles and miles of training, I honed my leg action to such a degree that I barely lifted my leg off the ground. The Clayton shuffle is probably the best thing that ever happened to my running. It was economical and easy on my body.

Clayton's observations are valuable. He points out that his style of running has idiosyncrasies (his upper body movements) that are unique and possibly counterproductive, but not worth changing. He instead identifies the more significant points—minimal knee action, a recovery stride that barely clears the ground. In addition, his stride has very little vertical motion. Efficient runners glide along without much bounce.

Learning to run with a smooth, efficient shuffle will protect you against overstriding. The longer your stride, the more you will bob up and down. And when you strike your foot out in front of you, it acts to brake your forward motion. With a proper stride length, the initial foot contacts the ground directly under the knee, not in front of it. The knee is bent throughout the movement and acts as a shock absorber, leveling any bounce or vertical motion.

Running speed is a combination of two factors: stride length and stride rate. If you shorten your stride length, you must increase your stride rate to maintain speed. To a point, increasing stride rate is better at increasing speed because it takes advantage of your muscles' elasticity. When a muscle contracts to absorb the downward movement at the point of footstrike, it is somewhat elastic. If this contraction phase is quick enough, as occurs in a short stride, the muscle can give this energy back like a spring at the pushoff phase. When stride length is long, the energy is absorbed and the muscle is less likely to spring back. Although we can consciously attempt to become economical runners, most experts agree that with training, people eventually settle into stride lengths that are the most efficient for them. But the bottom line is that it's better to understride than to overstride.

Other factors can also affect an economical running movement. Arms need to swing freely but in a generally forward/backward motion—a rather tight figure 8, not a circle or straight line. Allow your shoe, not the calf muscle, to absorb the impact at footstrike. Distance runners should never run on their toes. Finally, economical runners carry little if any excess body weight.

Running Posture

Proper running posture varies based on how fast you're going and whether you're climbing a hill. The faster you run, the greater your forward lean. For someone running at an 8-min mi pace, the forward lean from the hip is about 7 degrees. At 6 min per mile, this lean increases to 9 degrees. Sprinters lean between 12 and 15 degrees. Notice that the knee acts as a shock absorber by bending slightly throughout, as shown in Figure 5.1. If you keep the knee too stiff, an exaggerated vertical bounce results. Skilled runners have very little up-and-down motion in their stride. We

a   b

Figure 5.1 The body leans forward at a faster pace (a). At a slower pace, the body is more vertical (b).

all look to running downhill as a point of recovery. Indeed, it is easier on the heart and lungs, but traumatic on joints, tendons, ligaments, and muscle, especially in the hips, knees, and ankles. To lessen this trauma, bend the knees so they act as shock absorbers, don't lean back too far, and try to smooth out your downhill stride.

Running uphill requires several postural changes. You must increase your forward lean into the hill, work harder with the arms, and raise your knees to allow your legs to clear the hill. Figure 5.2 shows the uphill running movement. Runners often push off with the toes more on a hill than they do when running on flat terrain.

Foot Plant

As the foot is about to contact the ground, the outer edge is slightly lower, which means it touches the ground first. The footstrike usually begins with the heel making contact, but when speeds increase to about 6 minutes per mile or faster, it is quite acceptable for the foot to hit the ground somewhat flat-footed, or with initial contact at the midsole.

What normally occurs next is an inward turning, or rolling, of the ankle and then a roll forward, with a push-off coming from the toe box as shown in Figure 5.3. In a runner who underpronates, the ankle does not turn in enough. This allows a transfer of too much impact force to the

a

b

c

Figure 5.2   As this person runs uphill, he exhibits a pronounced toe-off and exaggerated forward lean (a), increased arm movement that causes increased work (b), and a high knee (c).

rear foot. In a runner who overpronates, the ankle rolls in too far, placing too much strain on the longitudinal arch (see p. 43).

Running shoes are designed with contact differences like these in mind. Faster runners should purchase shoes that have added padding for a midsole footstrike. See page 42 for more information on shoe selection.

Figure 5.3   At faster running speeds, the foot is more likely to contact the ground flat (a). Good heel contact during footstrike comes at a slower speed (b). After the heelstrike, the foot rolls forward.

Fresh-Run Training

None of us become economical runners without proper training. And the preferred method of training for running economy is to run moderately hard. Most runners actually run too fast during workouts, mistakenly believing that they haven't benefited from the training session unless they feel really tired afterward. The problem is that recovery from such all-out training takes a very long time, and it leaves the body in a state of constant fatigue. Running at a moderately hard pace should not leave you feeling stressed out. Chapters 6 and 7 are devoted to specific training programs for running.

Fatigued-Run Mechanics

It is one thing to execute an economical running technique when you're fresh and fully recovered, and quite another after a long swim and bike ride. We have done film analyses on runners before and after long runs, and what is most noticeable is the "bounce" in their strides. It appears that when the knee is fatigued, it is less able to operate as a shock absorber. The knee becomes stiffer, probably to protect against buckling and collapsing. So fatigue encourages poor mechanics by changing the natural action of the leg. Fatigue also encourages poor mechanics by distracting you from your focus (see chapter 9).

Fatigued-Run Posture

The fatigued runner also takes on a rather stiff upper body. The shoulders tend to hunch forward, and the arms remain tucked, close to the body. This tightness limits the freedom of breathing. An additional problem with hunched running is in the arm swing. An exaggerated side-to-side swing looks like an elbows-pointing-out rather than an elbows-pointing-back movement. This elbows-out posture causes the body to deviate from straight-ahead movement.

In the same way that pulling over the centerline in swimming causes you to go further as you "swiggle" through the water, side-to-side arm swing causes a wobble in your running mechanics. To prevent this, keep your shoulders back, and remember to swing your arms forward and back.

Foot Plant

In the fatigued state your lower leg muscles may not be able to produce the normal foot plant that they would in fresh running. To give yourself the best protection against injury, consider racing in your training shoes. Though lighter shoes allow you to run a little faster, they also provide less support, which forces your lower leg muscles to provide the extra support. This leads to a breakdown in running form, and when you have lost your form you waste energy. So training shoes can allow you to run faster when you are fatigued.

Fatigued-Run Training

As a triathlete, it is inevitable that you'll have to run when fatigued. And the best way to deal with this experience is to train in the fatigued state. The more you train while fatigued, the better your body will adapt and the longer it will tolerate fatigued running. An additional benefit is that fatigued training conditions your body to burn its fat stores more effectively. Regardless of how many carbohydrates your body can store, you still rely greatly on fats to provide energy. If your training program does not allow you to train while fatigued, your body will not effectively develop fat utilization.

Keep two cautions in mind regarding training while fatigued. First, do not begin fatigued training until your running movement is well developed and the distances required of you in competition are well within your capabilities. A very real possibility associated with fatigued training is injury, especially to the knees and hips. Second, fatigued training should be only an occasional, not a regular, part of your training program. Running under fatigued conditions can be very frustrating and discouraging, and most athletes can tolerate this on only an infrequent basis. We recommend fatigued training about twice a week.

The best method of training while fatigued is to combine cycling and running in a manner that simulates the actual triathlon experience. As soon as you finish a long bike ride, dismount, quickly change into your running gear, and head out. In your first few attempts you may make it only a mile or so before you quit, but you'll soon move out of this adjustment phase. It is very difficult for the body to reroute blood from cycling to running muscles. But by training this experience, the body becomes more efficient at the bike-to-run transition.

Recognize also that fatigued training is mental as well as physical. Few people are willing to commit to this type of training, but if you want to reach your competitive triathlon goals, you must include regular doses of fatigued running.

Part III

Training

The next five chapters teach you about your internal workings and provide tips for making your body stronger and sounder to meet the demands of triathlon training and competition.

Chapter 6 is a primer on training systems that helps you understand what types of training you must do to be successful in triathlons. You'll learn just what is going on in your body when you work out. Chapter 7 offers specific workout plans that you can use as presented or modify as you see fit.

Do you know what endurance athletes should eat? Chapter 8 addresses proper nutrition for strong and well-fueled triathletes. Have you ever wondered why you like endurance sports, or why the triathlon appeals to you? In chapter 9, learning psychology of the triathlon will help you set goals and stay motivated. Finally, nothing hampers the regularity of training more than injuries, and we discuss the most common injuries that affect triathletes in chapter 10.

Chapter 6

Training Systems

Endurance athletes spend a great deal of time doing sports that entail repetitive movements. Have you ever counted the number of revolutions in a bike workout? A quick estimate is 5,400 revolutions an hour! Because of this repetition, your workouts, whether in swimming, biking, or running, may lead to workouts that are similar in nature to the last swim, bike, or run you did. But the body doesn't benefit greatly from a constant stimulus. Its greatest benefit comes from variety.

Variety means changing the stimulus at the appropriate time to keep the body improving. For exercise to be of the greatest value to the body, you must practice different kinds of exercise. Different types of exercise produce different results. Our aim in this chapter is to help you achieve optimal results. We'll discuss the unique benefits associated with particular kinds of workouts.

Before we start our discussion of the particular benefits of exercise, let's clarify our understanding of the terms we use to describe exercise.

With this introduction to training principles, you will be in a better position to set up your own training program.

Training Principles

Fitness consists of the following four components: mode, frequency, duration, and intensity. If you can understand the four components, you'll soon see yourself training correctly. Let's look at these four components in detail.

Mode

Mode is the manner in which you do your exercise. An example is swimming. When you decide that your exercise is going to take the form of swimming rather than walking, biking, running, and so on, you have chosen the mode of exercise. This component is easy to understand.

Frequency

Frequency is the number of times each week that you exercise. For example, you may exercise Mondays, Wednesdays, and Fridays (three times a week). If you exercise twice on Monday (say, morning and evening), and once on Wednesday and Friday, the frequency would be four times a week. Again, this component is easy to understand. A triathlete is familiar with his or her frequency of exercise.

Duration

The amount of time it takes for a given workout is the *duration*. Did you realize that mileage is different from duration? Duration is a measure of time, whereas mileage is a measure of distance. Two endurance athletes covering the same number of miles could exercise for a different duration (period of time)—for example, a 5-min miler completes 4 mi in 20 min. A 10-min miler requires 40 min to complete 4 mi.

Intensity

The percentage of your maximum heart rate (MHR) at which you are exercising is the *intensity*. An example of expressing intensity is 70% of MHR.

To exercise at a given intensity you need the following formula: training heart rate (THR) = (maximum heart rate − resting heart rate) × intensity (percentage) + resting heart rate. For example, a person with a maximum heart rate of 195 beats per minute (BPM) and a resting heart rate of 43 BPM who wants to exercise at an intensity of 60% determines the training heart rate as follows: (195 − 43) × 0.6 + 43 = 134 BPM. See page 7 for a discussion of maximum heart rate determination.

Most people believe they know the intensity at which they are exercising because they know their pace. But pace is not a measure of intensity; it's a measure of velocity. A person cycling at the same pace on any two given days could be exercising at completely different intensities. One day, a person could be cycling at 20 mph in 50-degree weather at 60% intensity. Another day, that person could be cycling at 20 mph in 100-degree weather at 90% intensity. It's important to keep the concepts of pace and intensity separate.

Overload

An important concept to understand at this point is that of *overload*. Overload is what helps you improve your athletic condition. It means, in the most basic sense, that before you can enhance your ability you have to do something that creates a stress.

The first step, then, is creating a stress. The stress could be a longer training day, intervals at high intensity, or something else that your body has trouble handling. Weight lifters commonly use this principle; they increase the weight until it becomes too heavy for them to lift. The overload causes the body to break down in the sense that some damage to the body occurs. On the long training day this could be glycogen depletion. On the interval day this could be damaged cells from high lactate levels. A weight lifter may also experience fiber damage. After the stress, the body now needs rest. Without rest the benefit from the overload workout will be lost. Given a chance to rest, the body will not only recover, but will overcompensate for the stress it has received. This means it will prepare itself to succeed at the same task the next time you attempt it. The body does not like to fail. Be sure that the stress you apply to produce the overload is not too great. Injury can result when a great amount of stress is placed on your body. Your body needs to improve gradually, in small steps. This is a method requiring great patience.

Setting Up Your Training Program

Building a comprehensive training program is a difficult step that you must take before you can reach peak performance. In building this training program the endurance athlete must ask some questions—specifically, what, why, when, how, where, and who. This is not as confusing or difficult as you might think. Improved performance comes from proper training. Setting up the proper training program is a matter of determining the answers to these questions.

Questions to Ask

What should I do?   This is the first question an endurance athlete needs to ask and is the most difficult for the multisport athlete. It's harder to balance two or three modes of exercise than to focus on just one. An endurance athlete needs to know the details of a workout—the duration, the frequency, and especially the intensity that each mode requires.

Why should I do it?   This is where an understanding of training principles becomes particularly valuable. Without knowing why a particular workout affects your development, you will not know when your training has brought about an improvement, or when it has *not*.

When should I do it?   This question addresses the time of day a workout should be done, the order in which you should complete a combination of modes, and the time in a training year that a particular system should begin or end.

Most often, your schedule will determine the time of day you do your workout. You train when you have the time. A few considerations are worth mentioning if you have any flexibility in your schedule. Exercising immediately after waking places your body at the greatest risk of injury. The connective tissues of the body (tendons and ligaments), as well as your muscles, are in their lowest metabolic state of the last 24 hr, and you shouldn't ask them to achieve their highest metabolic state of the day in a short time. It is prudent to allow one hour or more from the time you awaken until you begin exercising. This also allows you time to eat something (see chapter 9 for proper nutrition). Exercising when it's dark outside poses safety problems, especially for women exercising alone. We advise training with a partner even if you think the area is safe.

The proper order for completing a combination of modes is important for the multisport athlete. If you are a triathlete competing in a standard-order triathlon, try to swim before biking and to bike before running. You'll improve your body's ability to make the transition from one mode to another.

In the next chapter we'll discuss the proper place in a training year to introduce a particular training system. Endurance athletes should realize by this point that they don't practice all the training systems all the time.

How is it best done? This question addresses the issue of specificity. We examined this area in detail in the biomechanics section of this book. Please refer back to chapters 3, 4, and 5.

Where should I do it? This question again brings up the issue of specificity. Think about where the race (or races) you're training for are going to be. Training correctly for a race may entail traveling a considerable distance to find the proper conditions (i.e., hills, heat, and humidity similar to those of the actual race course). Racing in a unfamiliar place can be difficult.

Who should do it? This last question also addresses specificity. Obviously, ultra triathletes will not have the same training program as sprint triathletes, and duathletes will not have the same training program as triathletes. More on this on page 140.

What Happens to Your Body

Many changes occur in your body during training. Though ideally all the changes will be positive (improving your performance), you must guard against the negatives.

During training your heart changes so that it can pump more blood in one heartbeat (improved stroke volume). Because your heart is pumping more blood per beat you achieve the same work load during exercise with a lower heart rate than when you were less trained. The increased stroke volume also will lower your resting heart rate. One negative change that can occur is overtraining, which results in an increase in your resting heart rate. Overtraining occurs when the body does not have sufficient time to recover, is given too great a work load to recover from, or is not given the needed nutrients to facilitate recovery.

Your skeletal muscles also go through changes during training. More carbohydrate (glycogen) is stored to allow for greater fuel supply. When more glycogen is stored in the muscle, more water also is stored there, because glycogen storage requires a 4:1 water-to-glycogen ratio. This means the endurance athlete experiences a slowdown in dehydration when this water is released (when the glycogen is used for fuel) and made available to the bloodstream. This is an added benefit for the well-trained endurance athlete, as dehydration is a constant foe in triathlons.

During training more fat is stored in the muscles also to allow greater fuel supply. The fat in your muscles provides fuel more easily than fat from fat cells (adipose tissue).

Also during training, more myoglobin is stored in the muscles, giving you a greater oxygen-storage capacity. The mitochondria in your muscles also increase in number and size. A further change is an increase in the number of capillaries supplying the slow-twitch fibers. This allows for more oxygen delivery and better waste removal.

Heat. It is likely that heat affects the athlete engaged in endurance exercise more than any other person. Athletes involved in exercising for short distances (e.g., 100-m dash) or in strength events (e.g., the shot put) prefer warmer weather. For an athlete involved in continuous exercise that lasts longer than 2 min, however, heat detracts from optimal performance. It can even place the body at risk.

The greatest risk is from heatstroke. Your body functions operate in a fairly narrow temperature range. When your core temperature reaches 104 degrees, these functions no longer operate normally. This situation can be life-threatening.

Although your core temperature may not approach life-threatening status, other forms of heat illness may affect you. Dehydration is a concern because your perspiration rate is increased. Adequate fluid intake is essential. The minimum amount is 24 fluid oz every hour you exercise. Diarrhea is also possible in high external temperatures. Besides the discomfort diarrhea causes during exercise, it also increases your fluid loss.

One thing about exercising in the heat is that your body does attempt adaptation. When you first face the heat, say in May or June when racing in northern latitudes, your body will show signs of adaptation in as little as 5 days. This is good, but you still need to take some precautions. Recommendations for training in hot weather include exercising before 10 a.m. or after 5 p.m. (avoid exercising during the hottest part of the day), wearing light-colored clothing (dark colors absorb more of the sun's heat), and exercising indoors if conditions demand it (extremely high temperature and humidity). Remember to factor in the stress that the outside temperature will add to your workout.

Training Specificity. The principle of training specificity states that you'll receive the greatest benefit from training when you duplicate the conditions that will occur when you test your fitness level (i.e., compete in a race). This principle covers a wide range of applications. For instance, training fast will help you race faster, running will help you do better in running races, and practicing on hills will help you in hilly races. Although these are all different applications of the same principle, you must examine each one for its particular benefits.

Periodization.   *Periodization* may be an unfamiliar term. Webster defines periodic as "having periods or repeated cycles." Periodization for the endurance athlete is the process of repeating cycles for improved performance. This translates to a training program that is at least threefold.

First, day-to-day training should be hard-easy (high/low intensity). Review our earlier discussion regarding recovery from hard workouts if this point is not clear.

Second, week-to-week training should follow some kind of progression (see Figure 6.1). One common progression is to divide four continuous weeks of training into a staircase. The first two weeks are the stairs leading up to the week of greatest volume, the third week. During the fourth week you do the lowest volume of training (a recovery week).

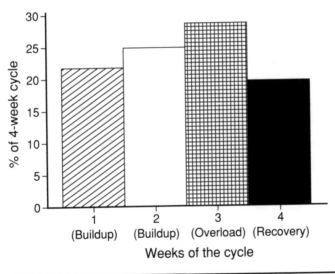

Figure 6.1   Periodization of buildup, overload, and recovery in a 4-week training cycle.

The progression should be in reasonable steps. For example, in the first week you should do 23% of the total amount you plan to exercise in the four-week period; in the second, 26%; the third, 29%; and the fourth, 22%. The progression becomes sharper as you approach the racing season, but not extremely so—for example, 22%, 27%, 33%, and 18%. Following a four-week cycle works well with a calendar, but you can use a three- or even two-week cycle.

Third, month-to-month training will also follow some kind of progression (refer to Figure 7.3 on p. 122). A low month of training might be 5% to 7% of the total you planned on training in a year, and a high month of training might be 9% to 10% of your yearly training total.

Recovery.   The term recovery is used in at least four ways in discussing training. The first is the time allowed after each high-intensity exertion in a workout—for example, 2 min of exercise at 90% MHR followed by 2 min of recovery exercise at 60% intensity. The second use refers to the time allowed between hard workouts. For example, if you performed repeated short bouts of high intensity exercise on Wednesday and competed in a race on Saturday, Thursday and Friday would make up your recovery days. The third use of recovery is in time of inactivity following an injury. The fourth use is the time used for restoration following the racing season.

Another possible use of the word recovery brings us to the concept of peaking. This means that the culmination of training is at hand and you will attempt a peak performance. In other words, you will try to have your best race or series of races. You allow your body time to recover from your training so that you will be in your best condition for a certain race.

Overtraining.   Simply put, overtraining comes from a lack of recovery. Remember that your body does not improve from stress alone; it improves from stress followed by recovery.

Some of the signs that accompany overtraining are elevated resting pulse rate, disturbed sleeping pattern, loss of normal appetite, and irritability. Any one of these is enough to tell you that something is not quite right; any combination of them is a sure sign that something is wrong. Other factors besides athletic overtraining, such as family or work stress and sickness, can also bring on these signs. No matter what causes these signs to appear, recovery must occur after they are present. Recovery requires either total rest (no workouts) or altered workouts requiring less time, less intensity, or both.

Do not overlook the importance of specificity to a multisport athlete's training program. Specificity encompasses both neuromuscular training and environmental factors. Improving neuromuscular pathways is one aspect of specificity training and is developed during specific workouts. Scientific literature has shown that swimming will not bring about better running performances, and vice versa. As a triathlete, you must train in all modes relevant to your racing. Although this is particularly true during the racing season, during the off season you can train by other modes.

Remember that you'll achieve peak performance by constructing first a solid base and then the upper stories. The base consists of improved maximal oxygen consumption and strength; this can be built by different modes than those you race. Cyclist Greg LeMond is an example of an athlete who changes his off-season training. By cross-country skiing in the winter, he achieves the same physiological goals—increasing maximal oxygen consumption and building strength—that he would by biking. With skiing, however, he decreases his chances of overuse injuries. As the racing season approaches, increase the training time spent in the modes you use in racing. During the racing season the greatest percentage of your training volume will be in the modes you race.

Your adaptation to the environment—heat, humidity, terrain, and distance—is another aspect to consider in specificity training. Adaptation takes place when you repeatedly expose yourself to an environmental condition. An athlete who confronts hot, humid weather abruptly will take at least 5 days to adapt to it. Similar results have been found for sudden exposure to high altitude.

Multisport Training

The minimal requirement for achieving the minimum level of fitness (any mode of exercise raising the heart rate to 60% MHR or greater for 20 min continuously, three times a week) applies in principle to each mode used by the endurance athlete. In other words, if you do not exercise three times a week in a particular activity, you will not become proficient at that activity. For example, you may in-line skate every Saturday. Even though you finished near the top of your age group in the local triathlons you entered, don't expect to have a strong level of conditioning for an in-line skate race. You just haven't trained enough for that. This may seem like an obvious point, but many athletes think any exercise will condition them for a specific performance.

Determining how much of each mode you need for proper training depends on the multisport event you have entered. In an international distance triathlon the relative percentage of time that each mode will take you in the competition should guide your training modes. For example, your 1.5-km swim time is 30 min, your 40-km bike time is 90 min, and your 10-km run time is 60 min. You should spend approximately 1/6 of your time swimming, 1/2 of your time biking, and 1/3 of your time running, except if you have a single-sport background with great ability or are noticeably weaker in any one event. Adjust the percentage of your training time to improve your weaker areas.

Of the three triathlon modes, running is the hardest on your body and can be scaled back to prevent injury. Your training program will seem more reasonable if your biking takes twice as long as your running. For those of you who are not yet thinking in terms of duration, that translates into about six times more mileage on the bike than running.

Types of Training

You now know the general guidelines of setting up a training program. Next it's time to discuss the types of training you should do. All of the following types of training represent physiological knowledge. We do not believe in promoting gimmicky workouts that claim to do "special things" for endurance athletes. Improved performance comes from correctly applying the types of training discussed in the following sections.

Aerobic Training

Aerobic training deals extensively with increasing your maximal oxygen consumption and your ability to train in a fatigued state. Aerobic training will make up the greatest percentage of an endurance athlete's training volume. You achieve aerobic training by doing *any* activity *continuously* for more than 10 min (although 20 min is usually the recommended minimum) *at an intensity equal to or greater than 60% of your maximum heart rate.*

Continuously means that the heart rate does not drop below 60% of MHR during the exercise. The upper limit for the heart rate is determined by the endurance athlete's tolerance to lactic acid. The maximal duration for aerobic training shows little limitation, for it can be performed continuously for well over 24 hr.

If anything limits the duration of aerobic training, it is carbohydrate depletion. For this reason, athletes should use some form of carbohydrate supplement for aerobic training that lasts more than 2 hr to prevent low blood-glucose levels. You must also take in adequate fluids to prevent dehydration in aerobic training lasting more than 1 hr. Aerobic training lasting less than 30 min is limited by little but produces little increase in maximal oxygen consumption. It is however, a good way to warm up for higher intensity training and strength training.

The benefits an endurance athlete receives from aerobic training are increased maximal oxygen consumption; an increase in the use of fat as a fuel source, which leads to a greater number of enzymes for fat metabolism while sparing carbohydrate stores; and an increase in the number of capillaries around the slow-twitch muscle fibers.

The risks associated with aerobic training mostly concern overuse injuries (see page 169). At highest risk are endurance athletes who increase their volume of training before their bodies have made the necessary changes to handle the increase. A gradual increase in training volume (see page 117 for actual guidelines), proper treatment of typical aches and pains, and proper use of recovery will minimize the risks associated with aerobic training.

The other risk associated with aerobic training is that you may not develop the neuromuscular pathways that you'll use when racing. You may have heard people who train hard every day say, "If you train slow, you race slow." This is partially true. If you train only at an aerobic training intensity, you'll never reach peak performance. You can alleviate this risk by practicing proper neuromuscular training (see the following section on speed training).

For the purpose of setting up a specific training program, we will call aerobic exercise that lasts less than 1 hr short aerobic training and aerobic exercise that lasts more than 1 hr long aerobic training.

Lactic-Anaerobic Training

Lactic-anaerobic training deals with increasing your tolerance to lactic acid and improving neuromuscular efficiency. The two types of lactic-anaerobic training are interval training and race pace training. Both types are high heart rate intensity workouts. The risk of injury and the stress associated with high-intensity exercise requires that you warm up for 15 to 20 min before exercise and cool down for 10 to 15 min following exercise. The warm-up ensures proper flexibility and preparation of metabolic systems. The cool-down ensures adequate transfer of blood volumes from the exercising limbs. We'll discuss interval training first.

Interval training for the endurance athlete falls into two categories: regular interval training and additional resistance interval training. The two incorporate similar physiological principles regarding their usefulness in training. Regular interval training occurs on flat terrain and in calm winds (or a crosswind) or in calm water. Additional resistance interval training is done on an inclined terrain, or against the wind, or both (on land); or in a swimming drag suit, or even against a current (in water). Additional resistance interval training helps you develop strength and neuromuscular efficiency on variable terrain.

You achieve interval training when exercising just below, at, or just above your lactic acid threshold (intensities of 80% to 90% of MHR). As mentioned earlier, this is necessary to improve your tolerance to lactic acid. In a person who is just beginning to train or is returning after a period of inactivity, tolerance to lactic acid may fall below 80% of MHR. Because of this lower threshold, such a person should expect the heart rate to be lower during interval training than when in a well-conditioned state. A few elite endurance athletes can tolerate lactic acid over 90% and need to adjust their training heart rates accordingly. The duration of exercise should be between 2 and 10 min with generally an equal amount of recovery time following the work interval in the 60% to 65% MHR intensity range (see Table 6.1).

The risks associated with interval training are great in that the presence of high lactate levels creates numerous hazards. These risks include the destruction of oxygen and fat-metabolizing enzymes. The enzymes cannot

Table 6.1
Estimation of Recovery Times Between Running Intervals

Loading	Running time (RT)	Recovery time	Recovery activity
Short speed (all-out) (anaerobic capacity training)	10 sec	3 × RT	Walking and/or stretching
	20–30 sec	3 × RT	Jogging
Long speed (95%-100% of maximal effort) (anaerobic capacity training)	30 sec	3 × RT	Jogging
	60–80 sec	2 × RT	Jogging
Speed + endurance (90%-95% of maximal effort) ($\dot{V}O_2$max to aerobic capacity training)	80 sec	2 × RT	Jogging
	2 min 40 sec– 3 min	1 × RT	Rest
Endurance (80%-90% of maximal effort) (anaerobic conditioning)	3 min	1 × RT	Rest
	4–20 min	0.5 × RT	Rest

tolerate the high-acid conditions that result from high-intensity anaerobic training. Paying attention to biomechanics (see chapters 3-5) during interval training will lessen some of the risk associated with this type of training. Remember that neuromuscular development is an important part of interval training, and you cannot develop the proper neuromuscular pathways with improper biomechanics.

Race pace training carries a great risk in that you are exposed to high lactate levels over a longer duration than in interval training. The additional benefit race pace training provides over interval training is that it gives you the opportunity to train in the fatigued state. The duration of exercise is over 10 min and has no absolute upper limit. The shorter the duration of your exercise, the higher the lactate levels can be over the tolerance level (maintaining your fastest pace for 1 hr). For duration over 1 hr the lactate levels will be under the tolerance level by definition.

Alactic-Anaerobic Training

You can think of alactic-anaerobic training as finishing-sprint or race-surge training. The alactic-anaerobic energy pathway provides energy over a 10- to 20-sec duration. Alactic-anaerobic training occurs when you perform maximal exertion over a 10- to 20-sec duration. You need to take precautions when training for alactic-anaerobic conditioning, even if you are using a heart rate monitor, because your heart rate will not respond instantaneously to increases in work load. You may have fully taxed the alactic-anaerobic energy pathway with your sprint only to see your heart rate be 15 beats per minute away from maximal heart rate. Your training would be repeated 5 to 10 sprints, once every 3 min for 15 to 30 min of an aerobic training day.

For the endurance athlete, the benefit is small from this type of training. Yes, it is nice to have a powerful finish at the end of a long race to pull ahead of a nearby competitor, but the risks of injury during sprint training outweigh the benefit. Only when your finish in a race is of vital importance (such as determining the difference between first and second place) does the benefit from alactic-anaerobic training equal the risk. Remember that it won't have much effect on your finishing time.

Strength Training

Strength training is an important area many endurance athletes neglect. The greatest benefit from strength training is the resilience it develops in your tendons and ligaments. Tendons connect muscle to bone; ligaments connect bone to bone. Neither receives the blood flow that the working skeletal muscles receive. Injury to a tendon or a ligament requires more healing time than an injury of the same degree to a muscle (see chapter 10 for the specifics). Strength training builds stronger tendons and ligaments than endurance training alone.

The other benefit you'll see from strength training is an improvement in synchronization and recruitment of the motor units used during strength training. This means improved efficiency (your energy is used in going fast, not in unnecessary movements).

The risks associated with strength training, from muscle tears and tendon inflammation, are greater than with aerobic training but less than with interval training. They result mostly from improper warm-up and improper form. A good warm-up for strength training is 10 to 30 min of aerobic training at 70% to 80% of maximal heart rate. We highly recommend that you seek professional advice on the use of strength training equipment when setting up your training program.

One drawback of strength training is the problem of specificity. Although improved synchronization and recruitment of motor units of the working muscles occur during strength training, some doubt exists as to whether most strength training movements mimic those movements the endurance athlete uses during racing. If the movement patterns are not similar, the efficiency you develop will not be beneficial to you during racing. To achieve the greatest benefit, try your best to develop a strength training routine that follows movements you use in your endurance activities.

Speed Training

The value of speed training does not have a physiological base but rather concerns the development of the neuromuscular pathway. The term neuromuscular training is appropriate because you do it to develop a good connection between the brain and the working muscles. Perform this section of a workout at the speed (pace) that you would attain in a short-distance triathlon. By doing so, you can practice the pace you'll be using during a short race without encountering the stress associated with maintaining that pace over a long duration.

This concept will be familiar to people involved in skill sports (golf, tennis, etc.). Skill-sport athletes want to "groove" their swing or stroke. Under the pressure of competition they do not want to get "tense" and "blow their shot." To the endurance athlete getting "tense" is working inefficiently, and "blowing their shot" is wasting energy. Remember at this point the importance of biomechanics from chapters 3-5. In particular, remember "Fatigued-Run Training" from chapter 5.

There are two kinds of speed training: reminder speed and developmental speed. Both occur during aerobic training sessions. You accomplish reminder speed by gradually increasing your velocity over a 10-sec period up to the pace you would use in a sprint or international distance triathlon, and holding that pace for 10 more seconds. This accounts for a total of 20 sec. If you have never raced in a triathlon and don't know what pace you would use, see Table 6.2.

Table 6.2
Estimating Your Triathlon Race Speed From Interval Training

Swim	Bike	Run
Decrease the minutes-per-mile pace that you have been using for your regular intervals by 10%—for example, reduce 33 min/mi to 30 min/mi.	Decrease the miles-per-hour pace that you have been using for your regular intervals by 15%—for example, reduce 24 mph to 20.4 mph.	Decrease the minutes-per-mile pace that you have been using for your regular intervals by 20%—for example, reduce 8:24 min/mi to 7:00 min/mi.

You should perform reminder speed once every 15 min over the course of your aerobic training session, which amounts to approximately 2% of the total duration of exercise. This small percentage of the total duration will likely be enough to stimulate the neuromuscular pathway that you would use during a race. There is no physiological development of the additional muscle fibers recruited at the reminder speed training pace; the duration is too short. The benefit is neuromuscular. This means that to gain any benefit, you must practice good biomechanics. This workout also provides a pleasant break from the monotony of a long aerobic training day.

Developmental speed occurs under more stringent conditions. The relative duration is still short compared to the aerobic training session. The preferred method of doing developmental speed takes place over a measured section—such as 50 m for swimming, 200 m for running, and 400 m for cycling. The pace for developmental speed is the one you would use in a sprint or international distance triathlon. If you have not raced before, see Table 6.2 for an approximation of racing speeds. If your pace is slow enough that you require more than 60 sec to complete the distance, reduce the distance by 25%. You risk accumulating lactic acid if the duration is over 60 sec.

You must determine what your race velocity will be in these different modes. Then you determine the amount of time required to cover the aforementioned distances. See Table 6.3 for sample calculations of developmental speed.

Table 6.3
Determination of Developmental Speed for Swimming, Biking, and Running

	Swimming	Biking	Running
Example of race speed	25 min/mi	21 mph	7 min/mi
Conversion factor[1]	0.037 sec/m	0.447 m/sec	0.037 sec/m
Speed	25 min/mi × 0.037 = 0.93 sec/m	21 mph × 0.447 = 9.39 m/sec	7 min/mi × 0.037 = 0.26 sec/m
Distance	50 m	400 m	200 m
Duration	50 m × 0.93 sec/m = 46.5 sec	400 m ÷ 9.39 m/sec = 42.6 sec	200 m × 0.26 sec/m = 52 sec

[1]Determination of conversion factors:

Swim and run: Minutes per mile (min/mi) to seconds per meter (sec/m) (60 seconds per minute) ÷ (1,609 meters per mile) = 0.037

Bike: Miles per hour (mph) to meters per second (m/sec) (1,609 meters per mile) ÷ (3,600 seconds per hour) = 0.447

Perform developmental speed accelerations about once every 3 min. This means that if it takes you 45 sec to swim 50 m, you will recover for 2 min and 15 sec until the next acceleration. The full 3 min counts toward your allotted time for developmental speed. For example, if you have 12 min of developmental speed to do during a long aerobic day, you will do four accelerations.

When you have performed developmental speed on a measured section enough to know what the intensity should feel like, you can move these workouts to an open area. For example, if you have been running developmental speed on a 400-m track, you can do this workout on a street or trail. Make sure, however, that you cover the same section exactly to ensure the distance is the same, going in the same direction to eliminate the effects of the wind. For example, say you're running on a trail and it is about 200 m from one tree to the next. Simply repeat the developmental speed training between these two trees for the length of time necessary.

Flexibility Training

Flexibility training is crucial to the success of any endurance athlete's training program. It can be difficult to work the time required to practice flexibility into your training program, because you may not consider flexibility training to be an integral part of working out. Scheduling time for your swimming, biking, or running is difficult enough. If your time is limited, you would probably elect to spend your last 15 min exercising instead of stretching. However, failure to practice flexibility training regularly (though not necessarily every day) will most certainly increase your chance of injury. A common injury among endurance athletes is a first-degree muscle tear, commonly referred to as a pulled muscle. This injury occurs routinely because the contracting muscle (the primary mover) takes the muscle that will cause the return motion (the antagonist) past the point of maximal stretch. A muscle taken past this point will tear. A classic example is a baseball player who sprints from home to first base and ends up with a first-degree tear of the hamstring. The quadricep has taken the hamstring past its point of maximal stretch.

You should stretch after your muscles are warm, because this is when they are the most flexible. Don't try to stretch when your muscles are cold; tearing occurs more easily in a cold muscle. Just after your workout is a great time to stretch. Stretching before your workout can lead to injury of cold muscles. You can warm up before your workout and then stretch, but this has not proved effective in preventing injury.

Warm-Up and Cool-Down

Beginning and ending your workout properly have much to do with the overall success of your training program. You may find it difficult to incorporate a warm-up and a cool-down into a workout that already takes a great deal of your time, but it is well worth the effort. The benefits a proper warm-up provides are increased flexibility in the working muscles and a gradual increase of the metabolic processes used for energy production.

A proper cool-down helps your body redistribute blood flow from the working muscles back to normal (where the torso receives a greater percentage of the total blood flow). All endurance athletes should be aware that any cool-down (even if you practice good form) can result in feelings of light-headedness if an insufficient amount of oxygen is delivered to your brain. If this occurs the proper procedure to follow is to sit down and elevate your legs above the rest of your body. This will allow the blood that has pooled in your legs to flow back up to your heart and be pumped up to your head.

Keep in mind that a passive warm-up, such as a sauna, whirlpool, or hot shower, is *not* capable of providing the physiological benefit that an active warm-up (one that uses movement) can provide. The best active warm-up uses movements similar to those you will be using during your workout. For example, the best way to warm up for a day of intervals on the bike is to ride your bike at a moderate intensity (60%–70% of MHR) for 10 to 20 min.

Chapter 7

Specific Workouts

In the previous chapter we presented the principles and systems of training. You should now have an appreciation of the physiology taking place in your body as it adapts to training. It takes more than just working hard to improve your athletic performance. You'll never see progress—in fact, you'll burn out—if your training consists only of going as hard as you can, as long as you can, every day. Improvement comes from properly applying a number of training systems. When reading this chapter you may need to review the training systems discussed in chapter 6. When you are finished with this section of the book you should be confident that your training will result in the achievement of your athletic goals.

Although in the previous chapter we introduced you to training systems, we did not give you a method for putting those systems together into a complete training program. This chapter provides two comprehensive training programs as well as specific examples of workouts. The best training program for you is one that fits your unique demands; however, a book like this has size limitations. Because we cannot address each individual's specific needs, we designed the following training programs to give you a framework that contains all the necessary components. It will be up to you to determine what minor adjustments you need to make.

So You Call Yourself a Triathlete

When setting up your training program you need to evaluate your present level of fitness. Knowing that you want to improve your performance is important. You probably wouldn't be reading this book unless you wanted to improve your performance. However, knowing the level of fitness at which you're starting your training program is more important. You'll have a better understanding of where you can go if you know where you're starting from. Also, you'll better understand the rate at which you'll progress. Finally, you'll be more likely to be realistic about your performance goals.

Though no two people are identical, it is possible to place endurance athletes into some general categories for the purpose of addressing their training needs. The following are some general categories that may apply to you and your present fitness level.

Just Starting

You are starting an exercise program for the first time. We congratulate you on your choice! However, you'll need to be patient with yourself and your training.

Have you ever read about elite triathletes' volume of training? One look at their training regimes makes your body ache. These athletes have achieved a high level of fitness through consistent training over many years. No one expects you to train like they do.

In the early stages of your training, you'll see great improvement in your fitness level. You'll feel that nothing can stand in your way of attaining top athletic performance. This rapid improvement in fitness is normal and possibly addictive. However, after these initial gains you won't see the same magnitude of improvement in your fitness level. This "law of diminishing returns" applies to all athletic training. A "couch potato" who starts engaging in 20 min of continuous exercise three times a week may see a 100% improvement in fitness level. Unfortunately, he or she will not see a 400% improvement when exercising 40 min six times a week, even though that is four times more exercise.

As a beginner you probably want to begin practicing all the training systems mentioned in the last chapter. As important as you believe this to be, you cannot use all the training systems immediately. Your body needs time to adapt before you subject it to the high intensity of regular and additional resistance intervals (see p. 105) and race pace (see p. 107).

Aerobic training, strength training, and flexibility training provide a good beginning regimen. Long aerobic workouts will stress your body enough to produce many physiological changes. Within a month or two you'll be ready to add higher intensity work. After you've begun training with the higher training systems and competed in a few races, you can move up to the intermediate-ability classification.

Starting Over

You are a triathlete who, either through injury or by choice, has been out of training for 6 months or more. Your road is not much different from that of a beginner because you have no carryover of physiological conditioning (although there is plenty of biomechanical carryover). Some people think that once you've been in shape, it's easier to get back in shape. But this is not true from a physiological standpoint. You need to be especially patient with yourself. It will take time for you to return to the level where you were previously.

One asset you do have is an understanding of your body. You've already worked with the three sports of the triathlon. You've also made the financial investment in equipment and clothing. Within a few months you'll be able to reclassify yourself as an intermediate-ability triathlete.

Intermediate Ability

Many of you will fall into this category. Unlike the elite endurance athlete, your athletic goals include finishing each race you enter, training to compete in longer races, and staying motivated to train regularly. You may not have seen your finish times improve for a while. You may have listened to endless, conflicting training advice. You may struggle to find enough time to train. You need to stay focused on the positives: You have a solid training base from which to work, experience at racing, training partners, and the determination that has kept you training for this long.

As a person with an exercise background, you stand to benefit considerably from a sound training program. You'll see improvements in race performances without having to train more. You can exercise injury-free. And you can still enjoy exercise as much as you ever have.

Elite

Few athletes will ever attain this level, but if you are one of them, it is important that you have a sound training program; otherwise you won't be able to reach your peak performance. You, of all athletes, have to be willing to train, for at least part of the year, on the edge. It isn't easy to push your body to its limits without overtraining. There's not much room for error—you might want to hold back just a little, yet you must be in top condition to race in a highly competitive environment. You'll be required to keep extremely detailed records of your workouts, to determine what is and is not too much stress. You may have knowledge of the information presented in the last chapter, but putting it all together may be the last step. This chapter is for you!

Single-Sport Background

Many of the first triathletes were products of single-sport backgrounds. This meant they had to learn two sports to compete in triathlons. Today, many beginning endurance athletes start their training with an understanding of the benefits of multisport training. Those endurance athletes start their athletic careers learning two or three sports (sometimes more) immediately. However, many single-sport endurance athletes still turn to the triathlon. The single-sport endurance athlete must learn to train equally for three sports, often struggling with the two new ones. It is wrong to assume when racing in a triathlon that an endurance athlete with a background in one particular sport has an edge over an endurance athlete from a different background. Though the first triathlons were dominated by people with swimming backgrounds (for example, Dave Scott), no one ever assumed that swimmers were naturally better triathletes. Neither was the triathlon world convinced that someone with a great cycling background (for example, John Howard) was a sure winner. The many single-sport endurance athletes learning the benefits of multisport training must not forget the activity that brought them into endurance sports, but must also realize that peak performances can come from any number of areas. The leading cause of peak performances in a triathlete is a good training program, not familiarity with any one sport.

A good training program begins with consistency. The human body gradually adapts to the demands you place on it during training. No single workout will bring you to your physical peak. You must work steadily toward the goal of optimal conditioning. With the information from the previous chapters you should be able to understand what makes the following training programs successful.

Year-Round Systematic Training

One approach to setting up a training program is to look at the entire year as a complete cycle. We call this approach *year-round systematic training*. The first author to write about this was Rob Sleamaker in his book *Serious Training for Serious Athletes*. According to this approach, the end of one training year is the beginning of the next one. For those of you who have been training for a number of years, this idea may be familiar to you. You probably start planning for next year's races as soon as the last race of the current year is over.

Year-round training does not mean that you have to kill yourself 12 months out of the year. It means simply that you look ahead to decide what you need to do now.

When looking ahead, you know that you want to be in good condition for the first race. To be in good condition you need to lay a solid foundation early in the year, and you'll want to know which training systems are most useful. We call the early part of the training year during which you build your foundation the *base* stage.

You'll want to know when to increase the intensity of your training. We call this transitional time of the training year the *intensity* stage.

You'll also want to know how to peak for the racing season and how to maintain the best condition throughout it. We call the period immediately before racing starts the *peak* stage. With these thoughts in mind, let's begin our discussion and systematically break down a full year of training.

Training Volume

The first step is to consider the investment of your time. We call this investment of time the *volume* of training.

As with any investment, you are looking for the largest return, the biggest payback. You learned in the last chapter that training involves many components, each with its own benefits and risks. Think of the largest return on your time investment as achieving your highest fitness level, or achieving peak performance. You bring this about by correctly allocating your training time into the different training systems.

To estimate the amount of time you invest in your training, think about how much time you train each week, and multiply that by 52 weeks.

Training an average of 7 hr a week adds up to an investment of 364 hr in a year! That works out to more than 15 days of exercise, and that doesn't include your commuting time or time spent preparing for and stretching after your workouts.

Don't feel that you need to exercise the same amount of time each day. Doing so would be like placing all your money in one financial investment. You'll have some days that are harder than others, and some that are easier to allow for recovery.

In the beginning of the training year the hard days may not seem hard at all to you because they aren't that long. But as you get closer to the racing season, the hard days will become similar to an actual race. In fact, the closer you get to the racing season, the harder the entire week becomes.

Keep in mind that no matter how strenuously you may like to train, you should never have more than three high-intensity days in one week. This is because you need one day for recovery after every hard effort.

The weeks that contain three high-intensity days constitute hard weeks. This is when you take an important step toward your peak level of fitness. This is also when you are in great danger of overtraining. The reason for this is that as you proceed from your beginning level to your peak level of fitness, the stimulus needed to provide an overload is greater. This applies particularly to your workouts that take place shortly before the race season.

Once the racing season arrives you'll cut back on the number of high-intensity efforts during the week. By not working out as hard during the week, you can channel that energy into your racing.

Training Stages

Even if you have a knowledge of training principles and systems, it is difficult to know how to put together a workout schedule for a whole year. To reach your highest level of fitness you must optimize each of the different physiological systems.

A progression exists that allows for this optimization. We can compare this progression to the construction of a building. Before you can reach great heights you must build a solid base. Each succeeding level must be built with the same attention to detail as the previous levels. The building that best represents training is a pyramid (see Figure 7.1). A pyramid has a large base and rises to a point at the top. Your training year must start with a solid base as well if it is ever going to reach a high peak.

The five training stages that allow you to reach your peak performance are base, intensity, peak, race, and recovery (see Table 7.1). Because we

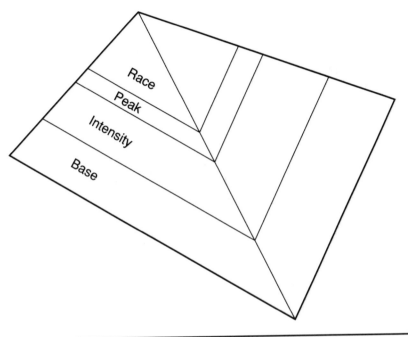

Figure 7.1   A successful training year must include four stages: base, intensity, peak, and race.

can look at one year as one full cycle, these five training stages make up a full cycle.

One year is generally 52 weeks or 364 days. To fit five stages into this time frame we can break down the training stages into the following amounts. Think of each 4-week phase as a period inside the stage. Using Table 7.1 as a guide, note that there are four base periods (comprised of 16 weeks), the four intensity periods (comprised of 16 weeks), one peak period (comprised of 4 weeks), three race periods (comprised of 12 weeks), and one recovery period (comprised of 4 weeks). Thus, the base and intensity stages are made up of four periods, the peak and recovery stages are made up of one period, and the race stage is made up of three periods.

Base.   Because the base stage is the first stage in each training year, it forms the base of the training pyramid. Table 7.1 shows that the percentage of the total training volume in the four base periods gradually increases from 7% to 8%.

Looking at Figure 7.2 and using 364 hr as your yearly training volume, you can see that the first base period would have 25 hr 34 min of training time and the last base period would have 29 hr 7 min of training time.

Table 7.1
Training Year Summary

Period	Training stage	% of hr/year	Periodization %				
1	Base 1	7.00	23	26	29	22	100
2	Base 2	7.00	23	26	29	22	100
3	Base 3	7.50	23	26	29	22	100
4	Base 4	8.00	23	26	29	22	100
5	Intensity 1	8.50	22	27	33	18	100
6	Intensity 2	9.00	22	27	33	18	100
7	Intensity 3	9.50	22	27	33	18	100
8	Intensity 4	10.00	22	27	33	18	100
9	Peak	8.00	22	27	33	18	100
10	Race 1	7.00	30	20	30	20	100
11	Race 2	7.00	30	20	30	20	100
12	Race 3	6.50	30	20	30	20	100
13	Recovery	5.00	25	25	25	25	100
		100.00					

According to a periodization of 23%, 26%, 29%, and 22%, the first 4 weeks of base would be 5 hr 55 min, 6 hr 38 min, 7 hr 24 min, and 5 hr 37 min, respectively (see Figure 7.3).

As you build your base, your workouts will have a higher percentage of aerobic training than at any other time of the year. Although the percentage of your training that is aerobic will never be less than 60%, during base it will be as high as 80% (see Figure 7.4). Reminder speed takes up such a small percentage of your total training time (about 1.5% in the first base period) that it is not shown, *but do not forget to practice it*!

Because you accomplish aerobic training at a lower exercise intensity than when you are racing, it is important to remind your muscles of the biomechanics of going fast. This is where you incorporate reminder speed.

Remember, the percentage of time you spend doing reminder speed is small. You will perform reminder speed once every 15 min by accelerating for 10 sec and holding that pace for another 10 sec. The total time is therefore 20 sec out of every 15 min. This accounts for 1/45th of your aerobic training days, which translates to 2.2% of an aerobic workout day.

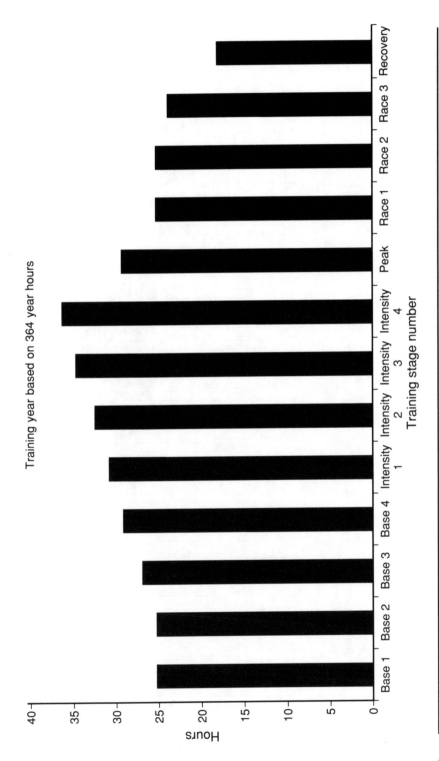

Figure 7.2 Hours per training stage.

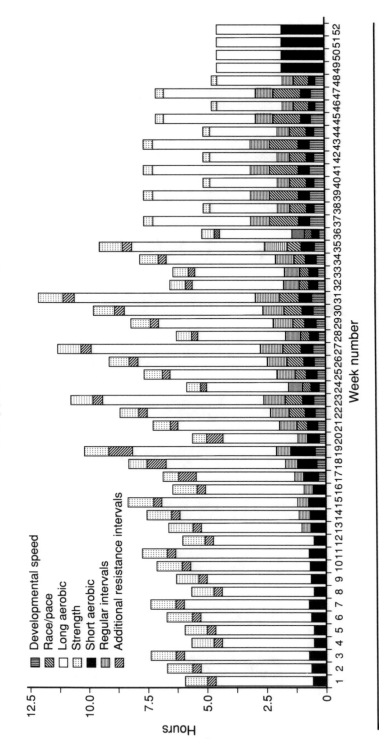

Figure 7.3 Breakdown of year hours by week.

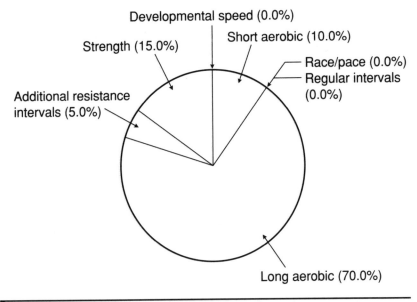

Figure 7.4 Breakdown of first through third base period components.

We recommend using a flat route on your bike-and-run aerobic training days. You want to maintain a steady heart rate, and training on hills will make it difficult for you to maintain an even intensity. Additionally, the risk of injury increases when you run downhill.

The strength training you do at this time will also be greater than at any other time of the year. Looking at Figures 7.4 and 7.5, we can see that strength training will account for approximately 15% of your total training in base. Don't forget to warm up properly for strength training—10 to 20 min of any variety of endurance modes.

You'll probably find that a health club is the easiest place to perform your strength training. Ideally, your health club will have swimming facilities as well, thus eliminating an additional expense.

During base, you perform additional resistance intervals to develop strength and maintain the fast-twitch muscle fibers. The fast-twitch muscle fibers are highly recruited at the pace associated with racing. The fast-twitch muscle fibers will atrophy if they are not worked. Looking at Figure 7.4, we see that additional resistance intervals will make up approximately 5% of the total training in base. This is a small percentage, but the intensity level is high.

For those of you who train in a flat part of the country, finding a place to do additional resistance intervals can be a challenge. If you have trouble locating a 1- to 2-mile hill that climbs steadily, or if bad weather eliminates

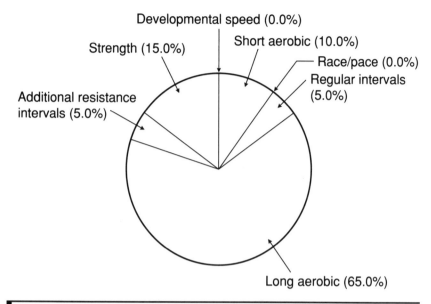

Developmental speed (0.0%)

Strength (15.0%)   Short aerobic (10.0%)

Race/pace (0.0%)
Regular intervals
(5.0%)

Additional resistance
intervals (5.0%)

Long aerobic (65.0%)

Figure 7.5   Breakdown of fourth base period components.

any location, you have other options. You can run on a treadmill, or you can put your bike in a high gear on a stationary trainer or use an exercise bike.

Table 7.2 provides a sample workout week for a triathlete training 364 hours a year (hr/year). As mentioned earlier, this is 23% of 25 hr 34 min, or 5 hr 55 min. If you have not been working out regularly, don't plan on starting at this point. Work up to this level of training volume gradually. Remember, 364 hr/year is an hour a day, and you can do less training if you want to.

Tables 7.3, 7.4, and 7.5 provide the sample workout weeks that logically come about from periodizations of 26%, 29%, and 22%, respectively. The 29% week should be a challenge, and you'll certainly appreciate the recovery week that follows.

By the fourth period of the base training stage, you are ready to begin regular interval training. Look at Figure 7.5 to see the additional 5% of your training time that is given to high-intensity workouts.

Table 7.6 provides you with the first week of the fourth base period for a triathlete exercising 364 hr/year. The noticeable difference between the first three base periods and the fourth is the addition of regular intervals on Wednesday. This means that you will only have two strength training days during the week, but they will be a little longer than previously.

Table 7.2
First Base Period, First Week Training Schedule

364 hr/year sample				
Day	**Mode**	**System**	**Intensity**	**Duration**
Sunday	Bike	Long aerobic	60%–65%	2 hr 3 min
Monday	Run	Short aerobic	75%–80%	12 min
	Strength	Strength	60%–70%	18 min
Tuesday	Swim	Long aerobic	65%–70%	1 hr 2 min
Wednesday	Bike	Short aerobic	75%–80%	12 min
	Strength	Strength	60%–70%	18 min
Thursday	Run	Long aerobic	65%–70%	1 hr 2 min
Friday	Swim	Short aerobic	75%–80%	12 min
	Strength	Strength	60%–70%	18 min
Saturday	Swim or bike or run	Additional resistance intervals*	90%–95%	18 min
Total hours:				5 hr 55 min

Total workouts: Swim = 2+, bike = 2+, run = 2+, strength = 3

*Saturday: Swim 3 × 3 min in a drag suit; *or* bike 3 × 3 min uphill, or into the wind, or both; *or* run 3 × 3 min uphill

Table 7.3
First Base Period, Second Week Training Schedule

364 hr/year sample				
Day	**Mode**	**System**	**Intensity**	**Duration**
Sunday	Bike	Long aerobic	60%–65%	2 hr 19 min
Monday	Run	Short aerobic	75%–80%	13 min
	Strength	Strength	60%–70%	20 min
Tuesday	Swim	Long aerobic	65%–70%	1 hr 10 min
Wednesday	Bike	Short aerobic	75%–80%	13 min
	Strength	Strength	60%–70%	20 min
Thursday	Run	Long aerobic	65%–70%	1 hr 10 min

(continued)

| Table 7.3 *(continued)*

364 hr/year sample				
Day	**Mode**	**System**	**Intensity**	**Duration**
Friday	Swim	Short aerobic	75%–80%	13 min
	Strength	Strength	60%–70%	20 min
Saturday	Swim or bike or run	Additional resistance intervals*	90%–95%	20 min

Total hours: 6 hr 38 min

Total workouts: Swim = 2+, bike = 2+, run = 2+, strength = 3

*Saturday: Swim 4 × 2-1/2 min in a drag suit; *or* bike 4 × 2-1/2 min uphill, or into the wind, or both; *or* run 4 × 2-1/2 min uphill

---

| Table 7.4
| First Base Period, Third Week Training Schedule

364 hr/year sample				
Day	**Mode**	**System**	**Intensity**	**Duration**
Sunday	Bike	Long aerobic	60%–65%	2 hr 35 min
Monday	Run	Short aerobic	75%–80%	15 min
	Strength	Strength	60%–70%	22 min
Tuesday	Swim	Long aerobic	65%–70%	1 hr 18 min
Wednesday	Bike	Short aerobic	75%–80%	15 min
	Strength	Strength	60%–70%	22 min
Thursday	Run	Long aerobic	65%–70%	1 hr 18 min
Friday	Swim	Short aerobic	75%–80%	15 min
	Strength	Strength	60%–70%	22 min
Saturday	Swim or bike or run	Additional resistance intervals*	90%–95%	22 min

Total hours: 7 hr 24 min

Total workouts: Swim = 2+, bike = 2+, run = 2+, strength = 3

*Saturday: Swim 4 × 2-3/4 min in a drag suit; *or* bike 4 × 2-3/4 min uphill, or into the wind, or both; *or* run 4 × 2-3/4 min uphill

Table 7.5
First Base Period, Fourth Week Training Schedule

364 hr/year sample				
Day	**Mode**	**System**	**Intensity**	**Duration**
Sunday	Bike	Long aerobic	60%–65%	1 hr 58 min
Monday	Run	Short aerobic	75%–80%	11 min
	Strength	Strength	60%–70%	17 min
Tuesday	Swim	Long aerobic	65%–70%	59 min
Wednesday	Bike	Short aerobic	75%–80%	11 min
	Strength	Strength	60%–70%	17 min
Thursday	Run	Long aerobic	65%–70%	59 min
Friday	Swim	Short aerobic	75%–80%	11 min
	Strength	Strength	60%–70%	17 min
Saturday	Swim or bike or run	Additional resistance intervals*	90%–95%	17 min
Total hours:				5 hr 37 min

Total workouts: Swim = 2+, bike = 2+, run = 2+, strength = 3

*Saturday: Swim 3 × 3 min in a drag suit; *or* bike 3 × 3 min uphill, or into the wind, or both; *or* run 3 × 3 min uphill

---

Table 7.6
Fourth Base Period, First Week Training Schedule

364 hr/year sample				
Day	**Mode**	**System**	**Intensity**	**Duration**
Sunday	Bike	Long aerobic	60%–65%	2 hr 11 min
Monday	Run	Short aerobic	75%–80%	20 min
	Strength	Strength	60%–70%	30 min
Tuesday	Swim	Long aerobic	65%–70%	20 min
	Bike	Long aerobic	65%–70%	45 min
Wednesday	Swim or bike or run	Intervals**	90%–95%	20 min

(continued)

▌ Table 7.6 _(continued)_

| | | 364 hr/year sample | | |
Day	Mode	System	Intensity	Duration
Thursday	Run	Long aerobic	65%–70%	1 hr 5 min
Friday	Swim	Short aerobic	75%–80%	20 min
	Strength	Strength	60%–70%	30 min
Saturday	Swim or bike or run	Additional resistance intervals**	85%–90%	20 min
Total hours:				6 hr 41 min

Total workouts: Swim = 2++, bike = 2++, run = 2++, strength = 2

*Wednesday: Swim 4 × 2-1/2 min, _or_ bike 4 × 2-1/2 min, _or_ run 4 × 2-1/2 min

**Saturday: Swim 2 × 5 min in a drag suit; _or_ bike 2 × 5 min uphill, or into the wind, or both; _or_ run 2 × 5 min uphill

You will perform flexibility training during the entire year, but here's a reminder: _Stretching after your workout helps to prevent injuries._ Don't risk interrupting your training by an injury. Flexibility training does not receive a set percentage of the volume of training, but consider 10 to 15 min a day a valuable investment.

Intensity. During the intensity stage you increase the percentage of the total volume of training. Table 7.1 shows that in the four intensity periods you gradually increase from 8.5% to 10% of the total training volume. This increase comes in 0.5% increments.

Looking at Figure 7.2 and using 364 hr as your yearly training volume, you can see that the first intensity period has 30 hr 56 min of training time, and the last intensity period has 36 hr 24 min of training time. With a periodization of 22%, 27%, 33%, and 18%, your last 4 weeks of intensity will be 8 hr, 9 hr 50 min, 12 hr, and 6 hr 33 min, respectively (see Figure 7.3).

Your body should adapt well to the increase in volume and intensity during this period. If it does not, you'll probably notice signs of over-training. If this happens, be sure to recover _immediately_! Continuing to work out will only set your training on a negative course leading to sickness, injury, and forced downtime.

The higher percentage of the total training volume allotted to intensity means that the longest aerobic days are in the last period. Some of these days may be difficult mentally, but they have a purpose! They'll help develop self-confidence.

It is important to begin some combined mode days by the end of the intensity stage. You are getting close to race season, and you need to practice making the transition from one mode of exercise to another. This means you should try swim-to-bike days and bike-to-run days.

Looking at Figures 7.6 and 7.7, you can see that the percentage of the total training in intensity that aerobic training consumes begins at approximately 70% and drops to 65%. This decrease in aerobic training allows for an increase in interval training, which allows you to develop a better tolerance to lactic acid. Remember that about 2% of aerobic training involves reminder speed.

Besides reminder speed, developmental speed training begins in the intensity stage (see calculations on p. 110). The percentage is small, approximately 5%, but valuable. You can do this training during one or two of your aerobic training days.

The intensity stage focuses on developing your threshold to lactic acid. This means increasing the amount of interval training (both additional resistance and regular) to approximately 15% of your total training volume.

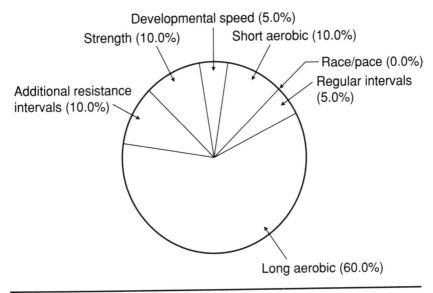

Figure 7.6 Breakdown of first intensity period components.

Toward the end of the intensity stage, you'll initiate race pace training. Race pace workouts are short, practice races that enable you to work out your prerace ritual (see p. 197). Race pace training takes over the percentage of training volume previously occupied by aerobic training. Because you still want two interval workouts during the week, you'll have to move your additional resistance intervals to Monday.

Strength training takes place twice a week during intensity (see Table 7.7 and 7.8). From Figures 7.6 and 7.7 you can see that the percentage is approximately 10% of the total training volume. Table 7.7 shows the first week of the first intensity period for a triathlete training 364 hr/year.

Table 7.7
First Intensity Period, First Week Training Schedule

		364 hr/year sample		
Day	**Mode**	**System**	**Intensity**	**Duration**
Sunday	Swim	Long aerobic	60%–65%	23 min
	Bike	Long aerobic	60%–65%	1 hr 40 min
Monday	Run	Short aerobic	75%–80%	20 min
	Strength	Strength	60%–70%	20 min
Tuesday	Swim	Long aerobic*	65%–70%	21 min
	Bike	Long aerobic*	65%–70%	40 min
Wednesday	Swim or bike or run	Intervals**	90%–95%	20 min
Thursday	Bike	Long aerobic*	65%–70%	40 min
	Run	Long aerobic*	65%–70%	21 min
Friday	Swim	Short aerobic	75%–80%	20 min
	Strength	Strength	60%–70%	20 min
Saturday	Swim or bike or run	Additional resistance intervals***	85%–90%	41 min

Total hours: 6 hr 46 min

Total workouts: Swim = 3++, bike = 3++, run = 2++, strength = 2

*Tuesday and Thursday: Includes 10 min of developmental speed training; see page 129

**Wednesday: Swim 4 × 2-1/2 min, or bike 4 × 2-1/2 min, or run 4 × 2-1/2 min

***Saturday: Swim 2 × 5 min in a drag suit; or bike 2 × 5 min uphill, or into the wind, or both; or run 2 × 5 min uphill

As always, you must practice flexibility training. You may find it difficult to take the time to stretch when your workouts take up so much of your time during intensity, but it is well worth the investment.

In the last three intensity periods you begin to practice race pace training (see Figure 7.7). This moves additional resistance intervals from Saturday to Monday (see Table 7.8). Use additional resistance intervals as your warm-up for strength on Monday. This is a tiring workout, but strength training is still too valuable at this point to practice only one day a week.

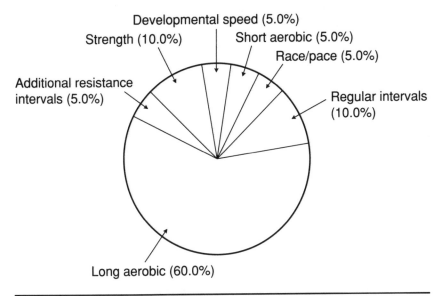

Figure 7.7 Breakdown of second through fourth intensity period components.

Table 7.8 shows the first week of the second intensity period for a triathlete training 364 hr/year. A subtle shift upward occurs in training volume; you are going to notice some physical changes. This is the time in the training year when you will see your resting heart rate decrease. Your percent body fat is also likely to drop.

Table 7.9 shows the first week of the third intensity period, and Table 7.10 shows the first week of the fourth intensity period for a triathlete training 364 hr/year. By the time you have finished the third week of the last intensity phase (a 12-hr week), you'll feel like you can handle any race!

Peak. The peak stage consists of only one period, but it has great importance. This marks the transition from training to racing. From Table 7.1 you can see that the percentage of the total training volume allotted to the peak stage is 8%, which is a reduction compared to the intensity stage.

Table 7.8
Second Intensity Period, First Week Training Schedule

		364 hr/year sample		
Day	**Mode**	**System**	**Intensity**	**Duration**
Sunday	Swim	Long aerobic	60%–65%	30 min
	Bike	Long aerobic	60%–65%	1 hr 40 min
Monday	Swim or bike or run	Additional resistance intervals*	85%–90%	22 min
	Strength	Strength	60%–70%	22 min
Tuesday	Bike	Long aerobic**	65%–70%	50 min
	Run	Long aerobic**	65%–70%	26 min
Wednesday	Swim or bike or run	Intervals***	90%–95%	43 min
Thursday	Bike	Long aerobic**	65%–70%	50 min
	Run	Long aerobic**	65%–70%	26 min
Friday	Swim	Short aerobic	75%–80%	22 min
	Strength	Strength	60%–70%	22 min
Saturday	Swim or bike or run	Race pace****	90%–95%	22 min

Total hours: 7 hr 15 min

Total workouts: Swim = 2+++, bike = 3+++, run = 2+++, strength = 2

*Monday: Swim 2 × 5-1/2 min in a drag suit; *or* bike 2 × 5-1/2 min uphill, or into the wind, or both; *or* run 2 × 5-1/2 min uphill

**Tuesday and Thursday: Includes 11 min of developmental speed training; see page 129

***Wednesday: Swim 6 × 3-1/2 min, *or* bike 6 × 3-1/2 min, *or* run 6 × 3-1/2 min

****Saturday: Examples of races or race simulations that you can attempt are swim 1,500 m, *or* bike 20-km time trial, *or* run 5-km road race

Using 364 hr/year as the training volume, the peak stage would be 29 hr 7 min (see Figure 7.2). This is a reduction in volume but not in the amount of high-intensity training. Aerobic training receives approximately 60% of the total training volume. Reminder speed still represents approximately 2% of every aerobic training day. Developmental speed still receives around 5% of the total training volume.

Table 7.9
Third Intensity Period, First Week Training Schedule

| | | 364 hr/year sample | | |
Day	Mode	System	Intensity	Duration
Sunday	Swim	Long aerobic	60%–65%	27 min
	Bike	Long aerobic	60%–65%	1 hr 50 min
Monday	Swim or bike or run	Additional resistance intervals*	85%–90%	23 min
	Strength	Strength	60%–70%	23 min
Tuesday	Bike	Long aerobic**	65%–70%	50 min
	Run	Long aerobic**	65%–70%	29 min
Wednesday	Swim or bike or run	Intervals***	85%–90%	46 min
Thursday	Bike	Long aerobic**	65%–70%	50 min
	Run	Long aerobic**	65%–70%	29 min
Friday	Swim	Short aerobic	75%–80%	23 min
	Strength	Strength	60%–70%	23 min
Saturday	Swim or bike or run	Race pace****	90%–95%	23 min

Total hours: 7 hr 36 min

Total workouts: Swim = 2+++, bike = 3+++, run = 2+++, strength = 2

*Monday: Swim 2 × 5-1/2 min in a drag suit; *or* bike 2 × 5-1/2 min uphill, or into the wind, or both; *or* run 2 × 5-1/2 min uphill

**Tuesday and Thursday: Includes 11 min of developmental speed training; see page 129

***Wednesday: Swim 6 × 3-1/2 min, *or* bike 6 × 3-1/2 min, *or* run 6 × 3-1/2 min

****Saturday: Examples of races or race simulations that you can attempt are swim 1,500 m, *or* bike 20-km time trial, *or* run 5-km road race

Interval training increases to approximately 20% of the total training volume. If at all possible, you should attempt to train in both the bike and the run. Doing interval training on the bike first and then the run will condition you for the critical triathlon transition.

Race pace training still receives approximately 5% of the total. The combination of interval and race pace training results in about 25% of

Table 7.10
Fourth Intensity Period, First Week Training Schedule

Day	Mode	364 hr/year sample System	Intensity	Duration
Sunday	Swim	Long aerobic	60%–65%	34 min
	Bike	Long aerobic	60%–65%	1 hr 50 min
Monday	Swim and/or bike and/ or run	Additional resistance intervals*	85%–90%	24 min
	Strength	Strength	60%–70%	24 min
Tuesday	Bike	Long aerobic**	65%–70%	55 min
	Run	Long aerobic**	65%–70%	29 min
Wednesday	Swim and/or bike and/ or run	Intervals***	85%–90%	48 min
Thursday	Bike	Aerobic**	65%–70%	55 min
	Run	Aerobic**	65%–70%	29 min
Friday	Swim	Short aerobic	75%–80%	24 min
	Strength	Strength	60%–70%	24 min
Saturday	Swim or bike or run	Race pace	80%–90%	24 min

Total hours: 8 hr

Total workouts: Swim = 2+++, bike = 3+++, run = 2+++, strength = 2

*Monday: Swim 2 × 5-1/2 min in a drag suit; or bike 2 × 5-1/2 min uphill, or into the wind, or both; or run 2 × 5-1/2 min uphill

**Tuesday and Thursday: Includes 12 min of developmental speed training; see page 129

***Wednesday: Swim 6 × 3-1/2 min, or bike 6 × 3-1/2 min, or run 6 × 3-1/2 min

****Saturday: Examples of races or race simulations that you can attempt are swim 1,500 m, or bike 20-km time trial, or run 5-km road race

the total volume of high-intensity training (see Figure 7.8). This is a high percentage of the total training volume, and you must therefore be alert to the possibility of overtraining.

Strength training receives approximately 10% of the total. Don't forget to use a short aerobic activity to warm up properly.

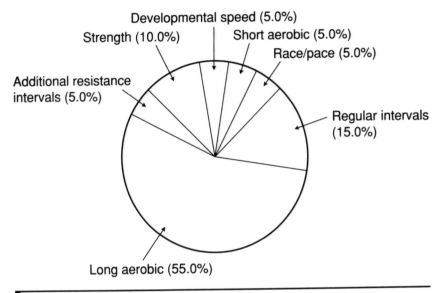

Developmental speed (5.0%)
Strength (10.0%)   Short aerobic (5.0%)
                              Race/pace (5.0%)
Additional resistance
intervals (5.0%)
                                        Regular intervals
                                        (15.0%)

Long aerobic (55.0%)

Figure 7.8 Breakdown of peak period components.

Table 7.11 shows the first week of the peak period for a triathlete training 364 hr/year. A noticeable shift downward in training volume occurs. You are now putting the finishing touches on your preparation for the race season.

It is crucial that you maintain flexibility training during the peak stage because of the high-intensity effort required at this time. Although you may not be able to see any visible improvements in your flexibility, you are still reaping great benefits. Stretching after your practice races is a good habit to get into.

Race.   The race stage is made up of three periods, each of which receives approximately 6.5% to 7% of the total training volume. In the example of 364 training hr for the year, this ranges from 23.5 to 25.5 hr each period. You can change the periodization in the race stage to a stress-recovery format—for example, 30%, 20%, 30%, and 20%—for the purpose of storing as much energy as possible for a big race. As the name implies, the emphasis of this stage is on racing. Race pace training now occupies approximately 15% of the total volume of training (see Figure 7.9).

Aerobic training occupies about 60% of the total. Reminder speed still takes up about 2% of every aerobic training day. Speed training now receives about 10% of the total training volume. This means that developmental speed is of a greater duration than during any other stage of the

Table 7.11
Peak Period, First Week Training Schedule

		364 hr/year sample		
Day	**Mode**	**System**	**Intensity**	**Duration**
Sunday	Swim	Long aerobic	60%–65%	20 min
	Bike	Long aerobic	60%–65%	55 min
	Run	Long aerobic	60%–65%	31 min
Monday	Swim and/or bike and/ or run	Additional resistance intervals*	85%–90%	24 min
	Strength	Strength	60%–70%	24 min
Tuesday	Swim	Long aerobic**	65%–70%	20 min
	Bike	Long aerobic**	65%–70%	43 min
Wednesday	Swim and/or bike and/ or run	Intervals***	85%–90%	58 min
Thursday	Bike	Long aerobic**	65%–70%	38 min
	Run	Long aerobic**	65%–70%	25 min
Friday	Swim	Short aerobic	75%–80%	19 min
	Strength	Strength	60%–70%	19 min
Saturday	Swim or bike or run	Race pace****	90%–95%	19 min

Total hours: 6 hr 35 min

Total workouts: Swim = 3+++, bike = 3+++, run = 2+++, strength = 2

*Monday: Swim 2 × 5-1/2 min in a drag suit; *or* bike 2 × 5-1/2 min uphill, or into the wind, or both; *or* run 2 × 5-1/2 min uphill

**Tuesday and Thursday: Includes 10 min of developmental speed training; see page 129

***Wednesday: Swim 6 × 3-1/2 min, *or* bike 6 × 3-1/2 min, *or* run 6 × 3-1/2 min

****Saturday: Examples of races or race simulations that you can attempt are swim 1,500 m, *or* bike 20-km time trial, *or* run 5-km road race

year. Try to include combination aerobic training days as frequently as you can.

Interval training receives approximately 10% of the total, which is generally all regular intervals. Additional resistance intervals have ended

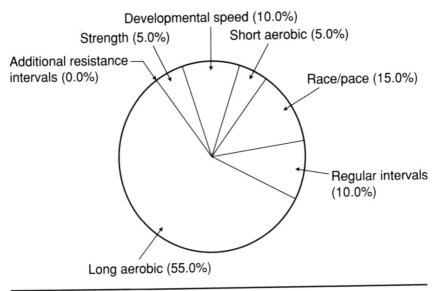

Developmental speed (10.0%)

Strength (5.0%)   Short aerobic (5.0%)

Additional resistance
intervals (0.0%)

Race/pace (15.0%)

Regular intervals
(10.0%)

Long aerobic (55.0%)

Figure 7.9 Breakdown of race period components.

for the training year, because you won't develop much more strength than you have at this point, and you want your legs to be fresh for racing. Remember to try combination interval days if you possibly can. Doing so will help your race transitions from swim to bike and from bike to run occur more naturally.

Strength training is reduced to approximately 5% of the total training volume. At this point in the training year, you're practicing strength training not for development but for maintenance.

Table 7.12 shows the first week of the first race period for a triathlete training 364 hr/year. The most noticeable change is a scheduled day off. It is likely that you have had a number of days off since you started training, but this one is by design and serves a purpose. Use this day to prepare for your race and store energy at the same time.

Again, don't forget flexibility training. Ideally, at this point it is a part of your everyday regimen. Stretching after a race is often the last thing on your mind, but stick to your routine; it'll pay off in the long run.

Recovery.   The recovery stage consists of only one period. Just 5% of the total training volume is given to the recovery stage. In the 364-hr training volume example, the recovery stage would be 18 hr 8 min, which works out to about 4.5 hr/week (see Table 7.13). Although it comprises the lowest volume of training of any of the stages, it is a crucial part of your training year. As we have discussed, you cannot see improvements in your performance without recovery.

Table 7.12
First Race Period, First Week Training Schedule

364 hr/year sample				
Day	**Mode**	**System**	**Intensity**	**Duration**
Sunday	Swim	Long aerobic	60%–65%	25 min
	Bike	Long aerobic	60%–65%	1 hr
	Run	Long aerobic	60%–65%	41 min
Monday	Swim	Short aerobic	75%–80%	22 min
	Strength	Strength	60%–70%	22 min
Tuesday	Swim	Long aerobic*	65%–70%	26 min
	Bike	Long aerobic*	65%–70%	1 hr
Wednesday	Swim and/ or bike and/ or run	Intervals**	85%–90%	46 min
Thursday	Bike	Long aerobic	65%–70%	50 min
	Run	Long aerobic	65%–70%	36 min
Friday	Off			
Saturday	Swim and/ or bike and/ or run	Race Race Race	85%–90% 85%–90% 85%–90%	1 hr 9 min
Total hours:				7 hr 37 min

Total workouts: Swim = 4+, bike = 4+, run = 3+, strength = 1

*Tuesday and Thursday: Includes 11 min of developmental speed training; see page 129

**Wednesday: Swim 6 × 3-1/2 min, *or* bike 6 × 3-1/2 min, *or* run 6 × 3-1/2 min

Table 7.13
Recovery Period Training, Weeks 1 to 4 Schedule

364 hr/year sample				
Day	**Mode**	**System**	**Intensity**	**Duration**
Sunday	Any	Aerobic	65%–70%	1 hr 22 min
Monday	Any	Aerobic	70%–75%	36 min

(continued)

▌ Table 7.13 *(continued)*

		364 hr/year sample		
Day	**Mode**	**System**	**Intensity**	**Duration**
Tuesday	Any	Aerobic	70%–75%	41 min
Wednesday	Any	Aerobic	70%–75%	36 min
Thursday	Any	Aerobic	70%–75%	41 min
Friday	Any	Aerobic	70%–75%	36 min
Saturday	Off			
Total hours:				4 hr 32 min

This 4-week period allows time for mental refreshment and physical healing. The components you use during this stage are aerobic and flexibility training (see Figure 7.10). Trying some different activities at this point in the training year isn't mandatory, but it certainly can be mentally refreshing. You can choose from a wide variety of endurance activities, such as in-line skating, cross-country skiing, aerobic dance, and canoeing.

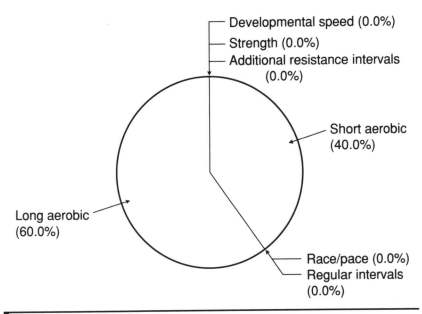

Developmental speed (0.0%)
Strength (0.0%)
Additional resistance intervals (0.0%)
Short aerobic (40.0%)
Long aerobic (60.0%)
Race/pace (0.0%)
Regular intervals (0.0%)

▌ Figure 7.10 Breakdown of recovery period components.

Training Toward Your End Goal

Undoubtedly, keeping your goal in mind at all times during training aids in motivation. Knowing exactly what you're working toward leads to straight-ahead progress. This process works well if you train with a particular race in mind. Many triathletes felt their first competitive stirrings while watching television coverage of an Ironman event. They worked their way arduously to the point where they too could participate in the great race. Other triathletes begin their careers when they hear about an international distance race that was held nearby. They discuss the race with a friend, and this leads to a decision that the two friends will train together to compete in the next year's race. To succeed with this approach, however, you need a firm foundation. Many endurance athletes never make it to the starting line of next year's race because of burnout and injury. Don't let that happen to you! Employ a proper training program. In the following pages we lay out a proven weekly training program for endurance athletes at any level of ability.

Working Toward the Goal

The sooner you start training for your big race, the better. The timetable we discussed regarding the year-round systematic training approach included more racelike training as the racing season approached. The same is true for success in end-goal training. If the race you have been thinking about is a month away and you have yet to do a combination training day, you aren't as prepared as you should be! Let's see how we can get you ready for any race you might want to do.

12 Months Until Race.   At this point you may have just finished a race and would like to do well in it next year. The first step is to take it easy for a while. This doesn't mean that you stop working out; you just cut back to a lower level, perhaps half the volume you were doing when you were at your maximum. Your body will appreciate the active rest tremendously. Take the opportunity to do different kinds of sporting activities, even to participate in team sports.

11 Months Until Race.   For you, 11 months to go before a race may seem like an eternity. It isn't easy to focus on a goal that's such a long way off. You have to break it down into smaller, more manageable goals. Talk to a Hawaiian Ironman participant and you'll likely hear about focused preparation. Such a triathlete knows how much swimming, biking, and running he or she should be able to do at this point. You should plan the same way if your goal is a long or ultra distance triathlon. You'll need the full 11 months to get ready.

At this point in the year, concentrate on building up to longer workouts. Aerobic training is your main concern. Also practice strength and flexibility training. Don't worry about high-intensity workouts. Although you shouldn't totally eliminate them, the training time they occupy should be relatively small compared to the rest of your training. Additional resistance intervals are a good use of your time. They help you build strength, develop specificity for races on hilly courses, and prevent atrophy of your fast-twitch muscle fibers.

You should be completing about 33% to 50% of the distances in Table 7.14 sometime in the next few months. This can be difficult if the weather is bad. Working out indoors can be a good solution.

7 Months Until Race. For the aspiring long and ultra participant, the time has come for higher intensity workouts. This means you'll spend

Table 7.14
End Goal to Race Long or Ultra Distance Triathlon

Day	Mode	Long	Ultra
			Distance in miles
		1.2, 56, 13.1	2.4, 112, 26.2
1	Swim	0.5 stroke drills 1.5 continuous	2.5 continuous
	Run	10	19
2	Bike	40	80
	Run	8	11
3	Swim	0.5 stroke drills 1.5 continuous	2.5 continuous
	Bike	45	105
4	Run	12–15	19
5	Swim	0.5 stroke drills 1.5 continuous	3 continuous
6	Swim	1.5 intervals	3 continuous
	Bike	34	55
	Run	8	19
7	Bike	50–65	100
Total :		Swim = 7.5 Bike = 169–184 Run = 38–41	Swim = 11 Bike = 340 Run = 68

more time on interval training and later on you'll begin race pace training. Also, you should start your combination workouts. You should be completing 50% to 75% of the distances in Table 7.14 this month or next month.

A triathlete aspiring to compete in an international distance race should be able to complete 50% to 60% of the distances in Table 7.15 in the next few months. Concentrate on distance, not intensity, but build up gradually.

4 Months Until Race.   One more month before the racing season begins! Excited? You'd better be. You still have considerable work to accomplish.

The sprint distance triathlete must begin training. You should concentrate on gradually reaching 50% of the distances in Table 7.15.

The international distance hopeful should be able to complete 60% to 80% of the distances in Table 7.15. Make sure you practice some combination workouts, especially bike-to-run.

Table 7.15
End Goal to Race Sprint or International Distance Triathlon

Day	Mode	Sprint	International
		Distance in miles	
		0.5, 12.4, 3.1	0.93, 24.8, 6.2
1	Swim	0.25 stroke drills	0.5 stroke drills
		0.75 continuous	1.5 continuous
	Run	3–4	6–8
2	Bike	13	25
	Run	3	6
3	Swim	0.25 stroke drills	0.5 stroke drills
		0.75 intervals	1.5 intervals
	Bike	15	30
4	Run	3–4	6–8
5	Swim	0.25 stroke drills	0.5 stroke drills
		0.75 continuous	1.5 continuous
6	Swim	0.75 intervals	1.5 intervals
	Bike	13	25
	Run	3	6
7	Bike	13–18	25–35
Total :		Swim = 3.75	Swim = 7.5
		Bike = 44–49	Bike = 105–115
		Run = 12–14	Run = 24–28

3 Months Until Race.   The racing season begins at last! The weather may not be beautiful yet, but the opportunity to go out and participate in some short running races should be a pleasant change. If local bike clubs organize some group rides (which amount to unorganized races), take the opportunity to join them and get in a good workout. See if you can get in some open-water swims; you'll notice a big difference from the pool.

The long and ultra triathlete should achieve the distances in Table 7.14 by this time, or certainly by next month. After that, your training volume should be shorter to allow for recovery. Doing a high-intensity workout during the week will help you stay near your peak without having to accumulate high mileage. Shorter races and interval training will accomplish this.

The international distance triathlete should also reach the distances listed in Table 7.15 by next month. Combination interval workouts of biking and running will prepare you well for the race.

The sprint distance triathlete should achieve 75% of the distances in Table 7.15 with 2 months to go, and 95% to 100% with a month to go before the race.

Reaching the Goal

Achieving a week like those listed in Tables 7.14 and 7.15 will give you confidence that you can do well. A word of warning, however: A week or two before your race is not the time to be logging this kind of mileage. In chapters 11 and 12 we'll explain in detail what to do the week before and the day of a race.

Chapter 8

Endurance Nutrition

Much has been written about nutritional concerns for a variety of individuals. Those pursuing a healthy lifestyle can readily find nutritional information in books, magazine articles, and videos. If you have a special nutritional need, such as diabetes, heart disease, or pregnancy, you have volumes of materials to choose from, and any nutritionist is well prepared to assist you. Even the nutritional needs of sport enthusiasts have been well documented. But for the endurance athlete, nutritional assistance of any type is sparse at best. This is a tremendous paradox in light of the great importance of nutrition to the endurance athlete. No other group of individuals has more unique nutritional needs yet less nutritional information available than endurance athletes. Nutritionists receive no formal training to serve endurance athletes, and books on the subject are virtually nonexistent.

To begin, let's distinguish between sport nutrition and endurance nutrition. Although you won't find these terms in the dictionary, the best way to recognize the difference is to consider the time you spend training and racing. If you train daily for less than an hour, compete in races lasting less than 1.5 hr, or both, then your nutritional needs can be met by sport nutrition principles. On the other hand, if you train daily for an hour or more in some kind of continuous activity (swimming, cycling, running, rowing), compete in races lasting about 2 hr or more, or both, you have unique nutritional needs that reach beyond the general guidelines for sport nutrition.

In this chapter we investigate the fuels the body uses in endurance performance, how the body obtains these fuels from the diet, and how it most efficiently uses these fuels. These concerns are extremely important to you as a triathlete because they directly affect your success in training and competition; they also can have tremendous impact on injuries and recovery from injuries. Too often individuals spend considerable time and energy striving for optimal exercise performance only to fall short because of inadequate, counterproductive, and sometimes harmful nutritional practices.

Essential Nutrients

Sport performance, as well as the everyday body functions of growth, repair, and even mental processes, can occur only when proper quantities of all essential nutrients are available for the body to use. The term essential means that the body cannot produce the nutrient by itself; therefore the nutrient must be supplied by the foods we eat. Essential nutrients consist of carbohydrates, fat, protein, vitamins, certain minerals, and water. Of these, only carbohydrates, fat, and protein provide energy-producing calories. Vitamins, minerals, and water are extremely important, but not as an energy source.

Energy Nutrients

Many people consider carbohydrates to be the main fuel in endurance performance, but in long-distance events, your body also uses protein and fat. In general, if the activity is intense and short, carbohydrates are the fuel of choice. If the activity is moderately intense and long, carbohydrates and fats provide the energy. But if the distances are so long that you run low on carbohydrates, then protein takes on the role of energy provider. This is an undesirable role for proteins because they better serve the body in repair, building up, and fighting infection. Because all three conditions apply to triathletes, a discussion of the dynamics of the three energy nutrients and how they interrelate becomes important.

Carbohydrates

It is well known that carbohydrates are the fuel of choice for short-duration, high-intensity exercise. This energy source is also the only one that the body can use for anaerobic activities such as sprinting, high jumping, and other field events. The most critical function of carbohydrates, however, is fueling the nervous system. Carbohydrates provide essentially the only fuel for nervous system function. That is why when you skip meals you begin to feel weak, light-headed, or nauseated.

The major problem with carbohydrates as the primary energy source is that the body's ability to store them is limited. Untrained persons carry only enough carbohydrate reserves to get them through about one day of sedentary activity. No wonder an inactive person becomes so fatigued when beginning an exercise program. With training, however, a person's ability to store and use carbohydrates is greatly enhanced, becoming as much as 2.5 times greater than that of a sedentary individual.

The storage sites for carbohydrates are in the liver (termed liver glycogen), skeletal muscles, and blood. The liver serves as a general fuel warehouse for the entire body; carbohydrates stored in muscles (muscle glycogen) provide fuel only for the muscle in which it is stored. Finally, small amounts of carbohydrates exist in the blood itself and are called blood glucose. Even in trained endurance athletes, only about 2,000 calories are stored in the form of carbohydrates. If you consume more carbohydrates than your body can store, the excess is converted to and stored as fat. Carbohydrates have about 24 hr to serve a need or find a storage site before they become fat. Once this conversion is completed, it is very difficult for them to be converted back into carbohydrates.

Plants provide us with carbohydrates. Carbohydrates are classed as either simple sugars or complex carbohydrates. The difference between these two substances is the number of sugar molecules that are bonded together. Simple sugars consist of either one or two sugar molecules. These can be single molecules of glucose, fructose, or galactose; or two of these can be linked, as in sucrose (table sugar), maltose (from grains), or lactose (from milk). But when these molecules are linked together in longer chainlike formations, they become complex carbohydrates or starch. Examples are potatoes, pasta, rice, and bread. Table 8.1 lists foods with high carbohydrate content from all four food groups.

Table 8.1
Foods High in Carbohydrate Content

Breads and cereals group	Fruits and vegetables group	Milk group	Meat group
Bagels	Apples	Ice milk	Black-eyed peas
Biscuits	Applesauce	Sherbet	Kidney beans
Bread	Apricots	Skim milk	Lentils
Cereal	Asparagus	Yogurt	Lima beans
Cornbread	Bananas		Navy beans
Crackers	Blackberries		Split peas
English muffins	Blueberries		
Gingerbread	Cantaloupe		
Grits	Cherries		
Matzo	Corn		
Muffins	Currants		
Pancakes	Dates		
Pasta	Juices and nectars		
Pretzels	Mangoes		
Rice	Oranges		
Stuffing	Papayas		
Thick-crust pizza	Peaches		
Tortillas	Pears		
Waffles	Pineapples		
Wheat germ	Plums		
	Potatoes		
	Prunes		
	Raisins		
	Raspberries		
	Squash		
	Sweet potatoes		
	Tangerines		
	Watermelon		
	Yams		

The type of carbohydrates consumed can be of great concern to the endurance athlete. When you consume simple sugars, the digestion process occurs quite rapidly, and the sugar enters the bloodstream very quickly. The body counters this ''gushing'' effect by releasing large amounts of insulin, which functions to remove glucose from the blood. The insulin released usually overreacts and leaves the blood glucose at dangerously low levels. Signs of fatigue, dizziness, and lethargy normally follow.

Exercising becomes a chore. Anyone who gulps down a chocolate bar or takes sugar (dextrose) pills immediately before training or competing should expect a poor performance. Consuming starch, on the other hand, generally protects against this sugar gush. Because of their more complex chemical makeup, starches need more time for digestion, and therefore they "trickle" into the bloodstream.

Fats

Fats provide the greatest source of potential energy to the body. Even people who carry proper amounts of body fat hold 90,000 to 100,000 kilocalories (kcal) of energy in reserve. Translated into performance, that is enough energy to run 1,000 mi nonstop if all the other body systems held together! Fats also cushion and protect many of the vital organs of the body, and the fat layer that exists just under the surface of the skin insulates us from the cold.

A function of fat that should be of great concern to the endurance athlete is that of glucose sparing. A trained endurance athlete's body develops the ability to sustain long periods of muscle contraction by deriving between 50% and 80% of its energy needs from fats. Whatever energy that fats can provide protects against the body using up its limited carbohydrate reserves. Certain conditions cause the body to use fats instead of carbohydrates.

The anaerobic system of energy production uses only carbohydrates for fuel. Whenever you begin exercising or push beyond your anaerobic threshold, you use carbohydrates exclusively. In aerobic exercise, fats and carbohydrates share the body's energy needs. After about an hour of moderate exercise, however, approximately 80% of the total energy needs comes from burning fats. This has tremendous implications for the triathlete who must sustain performance for many hours.

To create an efficient fat-burning system, you must train continuously for long periods below the anaerobic threshold. This training technique allows your body to become adept at pulling fats from the fat cells and processing them into usable energy. Stimulation by long-distance endurance training enhances all the critical fat-metabolism steps so that the transition from burning carbohydrates to burning fats occurs sooner and for longer periods.

The second concern, which may seem contradictory, is the evidence that fats need carbohydrates to be metabolized effectively. Exercise physiologists sometimes say that "fats burn in a carbohydrate flame." When carbohydrate reserves run low, your ability to burn fats is greatly compromised. So the next time you see a competitor take off in a spurt or breakaway, take heart; it's only a matter of time before you catch up again because of his or her carbo burnout.

Proteins

Protein's most important role will always be to serve as the building block of the body, especially during growth and repair. But we now know that proteins also play a role in providing energy when carbohydrate stores run low. In fact, protein can provide as much as 10% to 15% of the total energy requirements and as much as 45% when carbohydrates stored in the liver become low. This process takes place in the liver, which is capable of converting a portion of the protein chain into glucose. Because of protein's unique role, endurance athletes should increase the amount of protein in their diets. The recommended dietary allowance (RDA) for protein is about 0.4 g/day for every pound you weigh. An endurance athlete who trains daily and over long distances should increase this value to about 0.6 g/day per pound of body weight.

Even though you use protein for energy production and therefore need to consume more of it, the average person's diet contains about twice the amount of protein needed, which represents about 20% of all kilocalories consumed. This, coupled with the increased consumption of all foods that an athlete in training normally experiences, suggests that you're probably taking in adequate quantities of protein.

The quality of the protein you consume is also a concern. For a protein to be considered high quality, all necessary components of the protein chain, called essential amino acids, must be present and must be in the right proportions—a term called *biological value*. One food meets these criteria perfectly: the egg. So from a protein standpoint, the egg is the standard for protein quality against which we compare all other protein foods. Yet even though it's a perfect protein, as a perfect food the egg falls woefully short. This is because it contains high levels of cholesterol and fat and has virtually no carbohydrates.

Nutritionists generally agree that foods with biological values of 70% or more are of good quality. They advise eating a variety of high-protein foods to ensure that you get a complete complement of amino acids. Table 8.2 lists some of the most common high-protein foods.

One problem is that foods with high biological value might actually not contain much protein. For example, the egg is composed mainly of water and by weight is only about 14% protein. Some foods people normally associate with high protein content are mainly fat, such as meats

Table 8.2
High-Protein Foods

Food	Serving size	Protein (g)
Animal sources		
Egg	1 large	6
Milk	1 cup	8
Cheddar cheese	1 ounce	8
Yogurt	1 cup	10
Cottage cheese	1/2 cup	14
Codfish, cooked	4 ounce	30
Hamburger, cooked	4 ounce	30
Chicken, cooked	4 ounce	35
Pork, cooked	4 ounce	40
Vegetable sources		
Almonds	12–15	3
Peanut butter	1 tablespoon	4
Kidney beans	1/2 cup	7
Split peas	1/2 cup	7
Lentils	1/2 cup	7
Tofu	3 ounce	10

like ham, bacon, and hot dogs. Therefore, you must strike a balance between protein quantity and quality. In addition to the egg, the following foods are high in biological value, but low in protein: cow's milk (whole), fish, beef, soybeans, dry beans, peanuts, brewer's yeast, whole grain and white flour wheat, whole grain corn, brown rice, polished white rice, and the white potato.

Regardless of the quantity or the quality of the protein you take in, if your body lacks carbohydrates, it will sacrifice some protein for energy. Growth, repair, and defense against illness all become secondary priorities for protein when energy production is not being met by other sources. This is the reason that people who exercise without paying careful attention to nutrition often get sick or injured. The harder you train, the more important proper nutrition becomes.

Caloric Demands

Caloric demands vary considerably among competitors. You must consider such factors as body size, age, and environment. Steep terrains, cold and choppy water, and wind conditions all affect caloric demands. The energy you expend in exercise also fluctuates according to the intensity, duration, and type of exercise, as well your movement efficiency. A swimmer who knifes through the water, a cyclist with a great aerodynamic stance and pedal efficiency, and a runner with a smooth, comfortable gait will expend fewer calories than athletes who struggle every inch of the way. Use Table 8.3 to determine roughly the caloric demands of triathlon training and competing.

Table 8.3
Caloric Demands of the Triathlon Events

Activity	Intensity	kcal/lb/min
Swimming (crawl)	20 yd/min	.032
	45 yd/min	.058
	50 yd/min	.070
Bicycling	13 mph	.045
	15 mph	.049
	17 mph	.057
	19 mph	.072
	21 mph	.090
	23 mph	.109
	25 mph	.139
Running	11:30 min/mi; 5.2 mph	.061
	9:00 min/mi; 6.7 mph	.088
	8:00 min/mi; 7.5 mph	.094
	7:00 min/mi; 9.0 mph	.103
	6:00 min/mi; 10.0 mph	.114
	5:30 min/mi; 11.0 mph	.131

Data compiled from Cundiff, 1979; McCardle, 1981; & Whitt, 1983.

Experienced, dedicated triathletes may require as many as 5,000 to 6,000 kcal/day just to maintain their body weight, and a race such as the Ironman triathlon can call for as many as 9,000 kcal! Replenishing these calories is no small task, especially if it must be done on a daily basis. When your body's demand for energy becomes great, your diet must adequately replace these lost calories. If you don't maintain a balance between calories used and calories replaced, you'll experience more than just weight loss. For starters, performance often plateaus, which can quickly develop into overtraining. In this condition, you'll no longer experience the improvements normally associated with training. In response, you may train even harder, even though your body is actually calling for rest, recovery, and refueling. Many endurance athletes caught in this problematic cycle become so frustrated that they quit training altogether. If you continue training even while in an overtrained state, the problem can deteriorate to either illness or injury. Your immune system breaks down, leaving you susceptible to infections or viruses.

Non-Energy Nutrients

Up to this point we've been investigating nutrients with caloric value. But your body also needs another group of nutrients with different roles— vitamins, minerals, and water. These are essential to sport performance.

Vitamins

Vitamins are not food; they have no caloric value. People who take only a multiple vitamin at breakfast time do nothing to contribute to their energy needs that day.

Your body needs vitamins to assist in the breakdown of carbohydrates, fats, and proteins into usable energy. Vitamins also assist in constructing new cells.

With few exceptions, the body cannot make vitamins, and therefore they must be supplied through the diet. Few people realize that vitamins can be used and reused, and as a result you don't need to consume them in great quantities. But endurance athletes must realize one general concern about vitamins: The vitamins thiamine (B_1), riboflavin (B_2), niacin (B_3), pyridoxine (B_6), and pantothenic acid are all involved in the metabolism of carbohydrates, proteins, or both. Endurance athletes use these metabolic pathways extensively and should therefore double the normal consumption of these vitamins.

One other issue relates to vitamins and endurance athletes. Researchers have found that your body can lose water-soluble vitamins (B complex vitamins and vitamin C) when you sweat heavily. But this seldom justifies taking vitamin supplements. Increasing your food intake to accommodate your increased activity will give you those additional vitamins your body needs. But if you don't eat balanced meals, or if you avoid meats, leafy green vegetables, or fruits, taking a multiple vitamin is inexpensive nutritional insurance. But be sure not to take megadose levels of any vitamin. (A megadose quantity is one that is at least 10 times higher than the RDA.) In most conditions the body processes out excess vitamins. But when vitamin concentrations are extremely high, such as in megadose concentrations, the vitamins become harmful chemicals. Excess vitamin C—for example, 3 g a day—can raise uric acid levels and eventually create gout or possibly kidney stones. The best way to get all the vitamins you need in the right quantities is to eat a balanced diet. Endurance athletes typically take supplements for the B complex vitamins mentioned previously as well as vitamins C and E. Table 8.4 lists the fat- and water-soluble vitamins, their food sources, and the RDA for each. Fat-soluble vitamins are vitamins A, D, E, and K. Like the water-soluble vitamins, they are essential for proper health. The difference is the fat-soluble vitamins can be stored wherever fat is stored, and consequently do not need to be consumed regularly. None of the fat-soluble vitamins are required to be consumed in greater quantities by endurance athletes.

Minerals

Minerals, like vitamins, also play very important roles in carrying out the many metabolic reactions in the body. In addition, minerals are part of hormone chemistry: thyroxine (essential for proper body metabolism) needs iodine, insulin (glucose or blood sugar carrier) needs zinc, calcium is used in bone formation, and iron is needed in red blood cells.

All these mineral needs are relevant to endurance athletes, but, as with vitamins, a balanced diet supplies adequate amounts of minerals. An exception might be that active menstruating females need extra iron. They lose iron not only during the menstrual cycle, but also through sweat. In fact, men who sweat for long periods can also be deficient in iron.

Sweating can also result in an excessive loss of two electrolyte mineral salts, namely, sodium and potassium chloride. This problem can be especially serious in the early spring before your body has acclimatized to hot and humid workouts. Your body eventually adapts by protecting against these mineral losses, but it usually takes a couple of weeks. Electrolyte loss can cause heat cramps, heatstroke, or heat exhaustion. To prevent this loss, simply salt your food at meals. Taking excess salt in the form of salt tablets is not a good idea, because they contain extremely high doses of salt that can cause dehydration and hardship on the kidneys. You also lose potassium in sweat, but this seldom poses a problem as long as you eat a balanced diet. To protect yourself, eat a banana (a good potassium source) during long, hot training sessions.

Water

For the endurance athlete, the need for water far exceeds that for any other nutrient. Dehydration can kill an otherwise healthy person, and as

Table 8.4

Water- and Fat-Soluble Vitamins, Their Sources, and Deficiencies

Vitamin	RDA for healthy adult male (mg)	Dietary sources
Water-soluble Vitamin B-1 (thiamine)	1.5	Pork, organ meats, whole grains, legumes
Vitamin B-2 (riboflavin)	1.8	Widely distributed in foods
Niacin	20	Liver, lean meats, grains, legumes (can be formed from tryptophan)
Vitamin B-6 (pyridoxine)	2	Meats, vegetables, whole-grain cereals
Pantothenic acid	5–10	Widely distributed in foods
Folacin	.4	Legumes, green vegetables, whole-wheat products
Vitamin B-12	.003	Muscle meats, eggs, dairy products, (not present in plant foods)
Biotin	Not established. Usual diet provides .15–.3.	Legumes, vegetables, meats
Choline	Not established. Usual diet provides 500–900.	All foods containing phospholipids (egg yolk, liver, grains, legumes)
Vitamin C (ascorbic acid)	45	Citrus fruits, tomatoes, green peppers, salad greens
Fat-soluble Vitamin A (retinol)	1	Provitamin A (beta-carotene) widely distributed in green vegetables. Retinol present in milk, butter, cheese, fortified margarine

(continued)

▌ Table 8.4 *(continued)*

Vitamin	RDA for healthy adult male (mg)	Dietary sources
Vitamin D	.01	Cod-liver oil, eggs, dairy products, fortified milk, and margarine
Vitamin E (to-copherol)	15	Seeds, leafy green vegetables, margarines, shortenings
Vitamin K (phylloqui-none)	.03	Leafy green vegetables; small amount in cereals, fruits, and meats

a result it commands the respect of all who are active in the heat. Water loss during endurance exercise can be extensive. Marathon runners, for example, have been shown to lose up to 2 quarts of water per hour, which amounts to a 6% to 8% loss in body weight. From a performance perspective, body water losses of 2% result in some decrease in performance, and when losses approach 5%, a substantial reduction in performance occurs. Water losses approaching 10% of total body weight can lead to heat illness, heatstroke, even death. Refer to Figure 8.1 for the spectrum of dehydration.

To determine the amount of dehydration you experience during a workout, weigh yourself before your workout nude and dry, after urinating. Complete your workout, making sure you drink plenty of fluids throughout. Repeat this procedure after you finish the workout but before you shower. This simple formula will give you the total pounds of water you lost during the workout:

Preexercise weight − postexercise weight = pounds of fluid lost

To determine your percentage of dehydration, divide the pounds of fluid lost by your initial body weight and multiply this answer by 100.

When you exercise in the heat, some dehydration is inevitable. First, realize that the thirst mechanism is a delayed response. The thirst sensation is designed to kick in when water losses approach between 1% and 2% of total body weight. Dry mouth is the initial sensation that is supposed

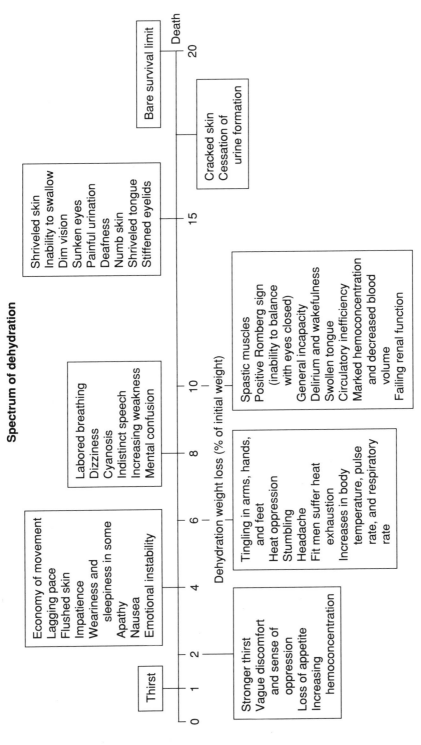

Figure 8.1 Spectrum of dehydration.

to signal you to drink. But the thirst mechanism takes its time gathering information from several areas of the body (mainly the blood), interprets this information, and responds accordingly. This means the endurance athlete might be dehydrated for half an hour before receiving the signal to drink. This delayed response can put you into a dehydration deficit that you are unlikely to exit until well after the race is over.

Another problem with dehydration is that the stomach can process only about a quart of liquid an hour during exercise. If you are losing more than this, you slowly exhibit signs of more severe dehydration (see Figure 8.1).

The prudent endurance athlete can do much to offset these losses. First, recognize that you are going to dehydrate, so begin drinking water even before you train or race. This is called *hyperhydration*. To hyperhydrate, you should drink between 8 and 16 oz of water no more than a half hour before you exercise. If there is more time than this between water intake and exercise, your kidneys will require that you stop and urinate along the way. Experiment with hyperhydration in your practice sessions to determine how much water you can take in.

Second, as soon as you begin exercising in the heat, consume 5 to 8 oz of water every 10 to 15 min to match the approximately 1 qt of fluid that your stomach can process each hour. Cold fluids (40 to 50 degrees F) empty from the stomach more rapidly.

One of the most important factors affecting the rate at which water leaves the stomach and gets into the body is the amount of sugar and electrolytes mixed in with the water. Sugar concentrations exceeding 2.5% can delay stomach emptying, and the body may not receive the water it needs as quickly. Beware that many commercial fluid-replacement drinks contain sugar concentrations over 5%. Sport drinks that contain glucose polymers or maltodextrins lessen this delayed emptying response somewhat. Read the labels.

The triathlete faces a need to replace both water and carbohydrates during exercise. In relatively cool and dry weather, you can increase the sugar concentration in your sport drink. But when the weather is hot, humid, or both, dilute these drinks or just use plain water. The problems of dehydration are more serious than those of carbohydrate depletion.

Diet During Training

The main objective in setting up a training diet is to ensure yourself adequate amounts of calories by consuming well-balanced meals. Not only does your diet need to contain enough calories to offset those you burn during exercise, but the type of calories you consume is critical. To determine if you are consuming enough calories, the scale is your best guide. If you are not overweight and not dehydrated, then you should eat enough to maintain your weight.

The type of calories you consume is a little more difficult to determine. Ideally, of the calories you consume, about 15% should come from proteins, 25% from fats, and the rest, or 60%, from carbohydrates. The best carbohydrate calories are the complex type (starches), not sugars. Fats should be polyunsaturated (oils) instead of saturated (solids). You should attain proteins from a variety of foods in an effort to take in all of the essential amino acids. In addition, you should distribute these calories evenly throughout the day, over at least three meals. If you need to consume more than 2,500 kcal (for women) or 3,000 kcal (for men), then the additional calories should come from carbohydrates. From a practical perspective, consuming large amounts of carbohydrates using only starches becomes very difficult. Inevitably, you'll consume some simple sugars (soda pop, candy, and cookies high in sugar) after your workouts. Granted, simple sugars can cause havoc in your body if you eat great quantities of them for long periods. Problems can include heart disease, diabetes, obesity, and dental cavities. But avoiding sugar calories completely when carbohydrate calories are critical is just plain impractical.

Consuming a high-carbohydrate diet during training is very important. Figure 8.2 shows how carbohydrate in the muscles (muscle glycogen) drops with successive daily workouts lasting 2 hr each. If your diet is low in carbohydrates, your muscle glycogen levels adopt a staircase appearance, and the overall level continues to drop. If on the other hand your diet is high in carbohydrates, the overall decline in muscle glycogen is avoided.

Notice that even when you consume a high-carbohydrate diet, your muscle glycogen levels never get fully restored between workouts. Only when you rest for a day does muscle glycogen level fully recover.

So what does a high-carbohydrate diet look like? Table 8.5 features sample meal plans ranging from 1,500 kcal to 3,000 kcal. As you can see, a 3,000-kcal diet includes plenty of food. Consuming a high-carbohydrate diet of over 3,000 kcal is difficult without including simple-sugar foods like soda pop and candy. What you also see in these diets is an effort to avoid high-fat foods. Not only are they bad for your health, but they contain twice the calories of carbohydrates.

In this chapter we highlighted the endurance athlete's unique nutritional needs. Just like with a high-performance automobile, the quantity and quality of the fuel you use directly affects performance. Neglecting proper nutrition inevitably will impact your success in training, put you at increased risk of injury and illness, and ultimately affect your performance.

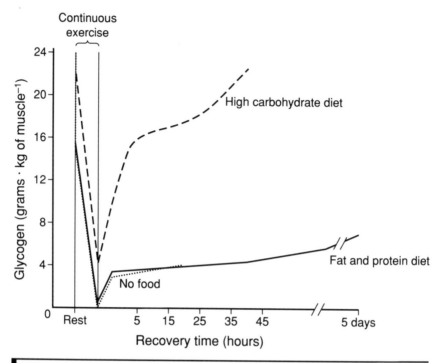

Figure 8.2 Rate and level of glycogen return in response to three different training diets.

Table 8.5
Sample Menus

Sample 1,500-Calorie Menu (Designed to Meet U.S. Dietary Goals)
Breakfast 1 cup cream of wheat with 2 tablespoons raisins 1/2 cup orange juice
Lunch 1/2 whole-grain pita bread 1/3 cup seasoned garbanzo beans with lettuce,   tomato, and onion as filling 1/2 cup cooked broccoli 1/2 mango 1 cup low-fat milk

Dinner

4 ounces lean beef
Baked potato with 2 teaspoons margarine
1/2 cup spinach salad with
　1 tablespoon French dressing
Yogurt shake
　1 cup low-fat yogurt
　1/2 banana
　3/4 cup strawberries

Provides approximately 56% carbohydrate, 17% protein, 27% fat

Sample 2,000-Calorie Menu
(Designed to Meet U.S. Dietary Goals)

Breakfast

1/3 cup bran cereal
1 cup low-fat milk
1 banana
1 piece raisin toast
1/2 cup grapefruit juice

Lunch

Tuna melt (use Pam or equivalent to grill)
　2 slices whole-wheat bread
　3 ounces tuna mixed with 1 teaspoon mayonnaise
　celery and green onion, chopped and folded in
　1 ounce cheddar cheese
　tomato slice
carrot and celery sticks
1 cup apple juice
1 cup low-fat yogurt with
　1 cup raspberries

Dinner

Stir-fry in 2 teaspoons oil:
　4 ounces chicken, no skin
　1-1/2 cups vegetables
1-1/2 cups brown rice
1 orange

(continued)

Table 8.5 *(continued)*

Snack

1 cup low-fat milk
1 blueberry muffin

Provides approximately 57% carbohydrate, 14% protein, 29% fat

Sample 3,000-Calorie Menu
(Designed to Meet U.S. Dietary Goals)

Breakfast

1 cup orange juice
4 pancakes
1/8 cup syrup
2 pats margarine
1 cup low-fat milk

Lunch

2 slices bread
3 ounces tuna
2 tablespoons lite mayonnaise
1 bowl lentil soup
1 cup low-fat milk

Dinner

1 breast chicken, no skin
1 large potato
2 pats margarine
1 cup peas
1 biscuit
2 tablespoons honey
1 cup low-fat milk

Snack

12 ounces soda pop
1 ounce candy bar

Provides approximately 57% carbohydrate, 18% protein, 24% fat

Chapter 9

Psychology

Veteran competitors acknowledge that sport success requires more than a highly trained, carbohydrate-loaded body. Amid the chatter at the finish line you'll hear expressions like "psyched out," "felt heavy," "choked," and so on. And for those who met their expectations, comments like "felt strong" and "got psyched" indicate optimum performance.

How much of a role the mind plays in attaining ultimate sport performance is impossible to determine. Coaches often say winning is 10% physical and 90% mental, but if that were true, why not spend 90% of each workout training the mind? The factor critical to optimal endurance performance is to recognize that we are psychosomatic (mind–body) beings. Mind-body illnesses—peptic ulcers, depression, some cases of high blood pressure—are clear illustrations of this connection. In sport, it is our mind that controls the muscle, not the opposite.

We believe that in every workout, mind *and* body are being trained. So you must develop the attitude of entering a workout fully intending to be in better shape afterward; if you can't, maybe you shouldn't do the workout. Training in mediocrity breeds racing in mediocrity. In this chapter we'll identify the proper mental attitude you need to take into your training workouts. High-quality, daily training of mind and body is the best strategy for achieving optimal race-day results.

Why the Triathlon?

Why are so many people attracted to this sporting monster named the triathlon as their personal "mountain"? If you cannot clearly answer this question, you are likely to wrestle with yourself every time you lace up your shoes or pull those goggles over your eyes.

Researchers classify achievers into two categories: people who choose tasks of intermediate difficulty, and people who choose either difficult or simple tasks. Individuals who are high achievers tend to perform successfully at any task they attempt; they are not attracted to tasks involving a high possibility of failure, nor are they likely to choose tasks that are ridiculously easy, for there is no satisfaction in doing something everyone can do. On the other hand, those who are less motivated to achieve choose tasks that are unrealistically difficult. They expect failure, and they give success over to chance.

The dynamics of the triathlon suit the high achiever perfectly. The three events—swim, bike, and run—are within the capabilities of nearly all of us. Effectiveness in each sport is mainly a product of consistent training, with only moderate reliance on chance. Given adequate injury-free training and some good equipment, the goal of finishing a triathlon is well within reach. Surprised to find so many successful folks taking on the triathlon challenge? To us, the challenge fits the personality perfectly.

Motivation to Train and Compete

A logical beginning for our investigation is to consider why people gravitate toward a sport that requires great sacrifices while offering small measurable rewards. For most, the motives to train and to compete are highly internalized. Unlike tennis, golf, basketball, and baseball, the triathlon carries little external reward. It's doubtful that a triathlete will ever be a highly paid media star. If your romance with the triathlon includes this fantasy, consider a different sport.

What really motivates a triathlete? The common thread that unites all rational-thinking humans is the need to achieve. Deep within us all is the motive to attain some internally defined standard of excellence, through either sport, profession, family, friends, or hobby. Often we carry out this achievement motivation by pitting ourselves against some other person or persons, but we can also fulfill this drive by competing against a set of personal standards. Thus, this standard of excellence can be internal (our personal level of aspiration) or external (achievement through competing against other people). Either way, it is important to understand that an individual's effort to constantly achieve certain goals in life is a fundamental aspect of personality and humanity. With regard to the basic human need to achieve, triathletes are no different from anyone else. We all know what mountain climbers mean when asked why they climb: The common response, "Because it is there," wells up in each of us, only in different ways and at different levels of intensity.

Attitude Is Everything

Another factor relevant to triathletes of all abilities is how you control your destiny in this sport. Many people believe they have little or no control over their success or failure. In their view, it doesn't matter if they try hard because they think they lack the talent to succeed. These people perceive themselves as helpless; when they do succeed, they attribute their success to luck, an easy opponent, or a lack of challenge. These people are developing the attitude of learned helplessness.

In contrast, other people embody the attitude of learned effectiveness. These people view weaknesses as exciting challenges to overcome and failure as a valuable learning experience that can contribute to future success. In short, they always find a way to increase their positive motivation. The main difference between the two attitudes is that those who practice learned effectiveness realize that perseverance and the self-discipline to work harder than others relate directly to success.

The implications of attitude for the triathlete are significant. First, very little in the triathlon occurs as a result of chance. Whether you're lucky or not, you cannot succeed without proper training and hard work. Second, you must be careful about how much you rely on technology to bring about success. Although good equipment is necessary, don't fall into the trap of thinking that technology is the primary factor in your success. Quit relying on magic potions and high-tech gizmos, and go for your personal best. Work hard at improving on your limitations rather than finding excuses.

Get Focused!

Sport psychologists who actively research the mind and sport performance arrive at one consistent observation: Successful competitors in all sports possess superior mental and emotional health. They consistently show fewer signs of psychopathology (mental illness) and lower levels of anxiety, neuroticism, and depression. They also show tremendous levels of psychic vigor—that "can do" attitude.

Does sport participation create this positive, narrow focus, or do successful athletes bring it into their sport? Most likely, both situations occur. A more important concern is how to alter your mental and physical environment to create such a focus. Probably the best way to improve your mental state is to reduce or resolve any problems that are irrelevant to the task at hand. Most elite athletes have achieved elite status because they expend very little energy on concerns that lie outside their immediate sport world. Corporate sponsorships allow these people to dedicate their days to training and to use the best equipment. With this in mind, it is easy to see how successful athletes can maintain a low level of tension, depression, and confusion—things that distract us from doing our best.

Most of us will never enjoy such freedom from financial worries; we must be content to work in our training programs around our other responsibilities. We can set realistic goals for ourselves—goals that are in balance with our other commitments. We can also attempt to eliminate things from our lives that create tension, depression, anger, and confusion. Finally, we can attempt to reprioritize our commitments, at least temporarily, in an effort to better focus our attention on triathlon training.

In a more specific application, practice narrowing your concentration or attention only to your body and your performance. Signals will come from within your body ("how am I doing?") and from the surrounding environment (fans in the stand, wind, heat, hills). Focus training is practicing which cues to respond to and which to disregard. Cues of boredom, comments from the crowd, excessive stress, negative thoughts, or an opponent attempting to psych you out are all detrimental to your performance; therefore, filter them out of your focus.

Arousal Versus Performance

We've seen people psych themselves before a big event, sometimes to the point where they nearly black out. We have also seen athletes get so worked up that they lose necessary control and concentration. Sport psychologists present this relationship as an inverted U curve, shown in Figure 9.1. In this illustration, performance improves as arousal increases; up to a specific optimal point. Beyond this point, additional levels of arousal actually create a deterioration in performance. Some athletes can reach optimal levels of arousal with very little need for "psyching up," but others might need to yell and scream. Athletes on the left side of the curve need to practice motivation techniques, whereas those on the right side must practice relaxation techniques such as stress reduction, deep breathing, meditation, or relaxation imagery to help them calm down.

In general, triathletes need to practice techniques that increase arousal levels. The most effective of these are goal setting, imagery, and thought control. Whatever techniques you use, effectiveness is very personal. A technique that works for your training partner might not work for you. It's important that you practice these techniques while training, not just during competition.

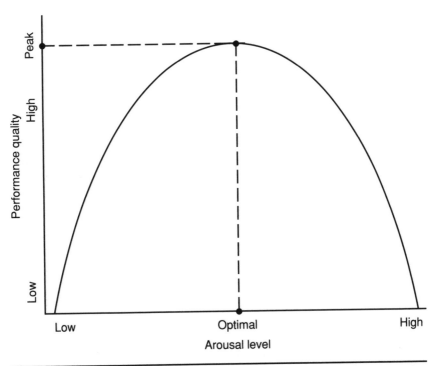

Figure 9.1 The inverted U hypothesis demonstrates the relationship between performance and emotional arousal.

Goal Setting

Nothing is more gratifying than meeting or exceeding a personal goal. By establishing realistic goals you are more likely to stay with your training program and compete at an optimal level. By contrast, setting unattainable goals will ultimately discourage you from training seriously and leave you with a sense of failure. It's better to establish conservative goals and attain them than to pursue unreachable ones. Establish both short-term and long-term goals. Eventually you might want to finish an ultra distance triathlon. What short-term goals can you pursue and attain that will help you build up to that ultimate goal?

Imagery

Imagery is the process of seeing in your mind's eye the perfect movement and visualizing yourself doing it. Can you see yourself executing each phase of the front crawl stroke using perfect form? Does it result in a frictionless glide through still water? The images you create are specific to the particular outcome you desire and are limited only by your imagination. Coaches often show their athletes videotapes of elite athletes executing a perfect movement. After several replays, they ask the athletes to visualize themselves doing the movement.

Thought Control

How many times have you talked yourself out of doing something? We all talk to ourselves many times during a day. Typically, we consider an idea, evaluate its consequences, and respond accordingly. For the athlete, positive thoughts about training and competing often increase performance, and negative thoughts almost always decrease it. And the longer we think negatively, the more likely we are to fulfill those negative thoughts. Thought control is the process of replacing negative thoughts with positive ones. For some, words such as *go, get it done, let's hammer* are quite energizing. If you bathe your thinking in positive thoughts, you'll likely wash away the negatives.

Undoubtedly, the mind plays a critical role in successful training and competition. We maintain that the mental discipline you develop in training will carry over into your competitive performance. Concentrate while training. Focus while training. Isolate your negative thoughts while training. Think positively while training. You need to train the mind and the body at the same time. By doing so, you will be ready both physically and mentally when it comes to performing in the big event.

Chapter 10

Injuries

Many endurance athletes suffering from injuries cannot remember the day their injuries began. What they do remember is the training time they missed because of an injury. The continual application of a force leads to overuse injuries, and endurance athletes' injuries usually stem from overuse. Working muscles produce force, which allows movement. The forces that cause overuse injuries are a part of training. It is possible, however, to avoid injury when training.

Injury Prevention

There is nothing like an injury to defeat your goals, challenges, and outlook on life. Some of the most miserable people to be around are athletes that cannot train because of an injury. So much of an athlete's identity is wrapped up in pursuing intense physical goals. To the endurance athlete, the dream is inevitably one of winning, improving, or at least finishing. Injuries cut deep into fulfilling these dreams.

Endurance athletes often get so caught up in pursuing these dreams that they overlook injury prevention. As with an automobile, most of us tend to fix the broken parts rather than follow any consistent plan of preventive maintenance. The irony of the situation, though, is that you can do a great deal to prevent injuries from occurring in the first place. Some athletes never get injured. Certainly genetic makeup affects injuries and injury prevention, but more importantly, you create your own injury destiny. Therefore, in this section of the book we outline a plan to help you move through your season of training and competition injury-free.

Injury prevention has five levels. Each level builds on the previous one, so make sure you resolve the concerns at each level before moving on to the next. The levels are as follows:

Level 1: Equipment

Level 2: Proper biomechanics

Level 3: Proper training

Level 4: Self-treatment

Level 5: Professional treatment

Level 1: Equipment

Before you first step down on the pedals or put one foot in front of the other, you need to make sure your equipment is in good repair and is properly adjusted. Wearing shoes that are worn out, not fitted properly, or not designed for your particular needs will almost certainly promote injuries.

Use a bicycle that is set up for your particular anatomy. Using a bike that is too big or too small will force your body into an abnormal position. Using a bike that is not adjusted properly will do the same. If you wear cleated cycling shoes, make sure the cleat is precisely adjusted; even the most minute maladjustments can cause knee problems. See chapter 2 for how to select running and cycling shoes, as well as the sections on bicycle selection and adjustments.

Level 2: Proper Biomechanics

Once you are properly outfitted, your next concern is refining the movements you intend to use in training. Chapters 3, 4, and 5 devote much attention to executing the proper swim, bike, and run movements. Training and competing with poor form create more opportunities for injuries. Use proper movement mechanics early on in your training so you will not practice and perfect an improper style of locomotion.

Level 3: Proper Training

Chapters 6 and 7 emphasized the need to progress gradually, to get proper rest, and to be alert to the signs of overtraining. These are all very important concerns that affect injury prevention tremendously. Progression, for instance, can be deceiving because the cardiovascular system often adapts at a faster rate than bones, joints, tendons, and ligaments do. Although your mind and physical signs may be telling you to move ahead, your joints have no way of communicating to you to stop until it's too late. Make sure your progression is gradual and calculated. Progression in 10% intervals per week is prudent.

Another suggestion is to stagger-start your training program. Beginning your running and cycling training at the same time causes tremendous trauma to the lower legs. Allowing skeletal and muscular systems to adapt to one event before introducing the next certainly decreases your chances of injury.

Finally, the prudent athlete learns to listen to his or her body. So many serious injuries occur because a person fails to heed the body's warning signs. The most obvious of these warning signs are swelling, soreness, and pain. Swelling is generally easy to detect. The swollen site is usually red, puffy, and warmer than the rest of the body. Swelling is a sure sign of injury and should not be neglected.

Soreness and pain may seem synonymous, but there is a distinction between them. Soreness is a natural response by the body whenever it is exposed to a new or higher than normal degree of physical exertion. We all experience soreness at the onset of our training programs. For the triathlete, soreness is at least a threefold experience in response to triple training. *Delayed* soreness is usually felt 24 to 48 hr after exercise. We can only speculate as to the cause of delayed soreness; the most plausible explanation is injury to the tendons and muscle sheaths that wrap each muscle completely and also wrap smaller bundles within the muscle. *Acute* soreness is another type of soreness you feel during exercise. You can identify this as a burning sensation, which in reality means that the mitochondria of the exercising muscle are receiving an inadequate supply of oxygen. Lactic acid is produced in such circumstances. Both types of soreness are a natural outcome of exercise and should not be viewed as a problem leading to injury.

Pain, on the other hand, is a body response that signals injury or potential injury. Pain receptors are built within the joints and muscles of the body, and these sense tissue damage occurring throughout the body. Pain serves as a warning sign and should be viewed as a protective mechanism. Realize that pain is a very relative issue, and your personality can affect your perception of pain, particularly the degree to which you accept or deny its presence.

Table 10.1 classifies pain into three degrees and guides you through appropriate treatment. Trying to train through pain is a crazy idea. You can train through annoying sensations, but not pain. Pain is destruction. It is time for athletes to trade in the phrase "no pain, no gain" for a more prudent approach.

Level 4: Self-Treatment

You can self-diagnose some injuries and treat them without incurring the expense of professional intervention. Such injuries include sprains, strains, tendinitis, and blisters that are at the first-degree level of pain. To treat minor sprains, strains, and tendinitis, reduce training intensity, duration,

Table 10.1
Pain Reference Table

	First degree	Second degree	Third degree
Symptom	Pain remains constant or increases during exercise without an alteration in form.	Mild pain during easy workouts, severe pain during hard workouts, resulting in an alteration of form.	Impossible to exercise without an alteration of form.
Treatment	Eliminate the exercise that increases the pain. It is reasonable to continue to exercise if *no* alteration of form results.	Slowly and cautiously, start the exercise that causes the pain. Continue exercising only as vigorously as proper form allows.	Eliminate the exercise for 1 week to several months. Experiment during this time with trial workouts to see if pain has been reduced or eliminated.

and frequency; then apply cold to the injury site and take ibuprofen (or possibly aspirin) to reduce swelling and pain. Blisters are caused by friction; to treat a blister, you need to identify and correct the cause of friction. Make sure you wear shoes that fit well and socks that fit snugly and are clean and free of holes or ridges. Smear petroleum jelly over any developing "hot spots." You can puncture a simple blister with a sterilized needle, carefully drain it, and cover it with a sterile dressing.

Level 5: Professional Treatment

Endurance athletes are usually reluctant to seek professional help, because by doing so they feel some sense of failure or embarrassment. The typical response, therefore, is to avoid making an appointment and hope the pain goes away. Rarely does this occur, however, and the endurance athlete continues to make matters worse. If you do seek medical help for an injury, you'll find that doctors who treat athletes often make a diagnosis and prescribe a home treatment program. They seldom direct you to terminate all training. Medical professionals are becoming more aware that endurance athletes are unwilling to become inactive, and they usually offer alternative exercises.

In general, any second- or third-degree pain should be diagnosed by a professional. It's better to deal with a relatively minor injury than to continue pushing until the injury is full-blown. Knee pain, if you cannot relieve it by adjusting your equipment or through biomechanics treatment (levels 1 and 2), warrants immediate professional referral.

You can seek professional help from a number of people. Athletic trainers are always a great source. If the problem is too complex, a trainer will often refer you to a team physician or an orthopedic surgeon. Most of these professionals are sensitive to an athlete's ever-present desire to continue training but experienced enough to tell the injured person the truth, not what he or she wants to hear.

Types of Injuries

The following look at injuries is not meant to be a comprehensive guide to injury treatment. It provides an understanding of how injuries start and where they can end up.

The RICE method is a practical treatment for many injuries. You can begin self-treatment using this method by following this procedure:

R = Rest; avoid the activity that caused the injury.

I = Ice; cold will reduce the blood flow, thereby decreasing inflammation.

C = Compression; holding ice on the injury site with some type of wrap that produces compression will increase the effectiveness of the cold in reducing inflammation.

E = Elevation; elevating an injured limb above the level of the heart will decrease the tendency of the blood to pool, thereby decreasing some of the inflammation at the injury site.

Injury to a Muscle

The most common injury to a muscle is tearing. Let's consider the three degrees of muscle tears. A first-degree muscle tear is commonly known as a pulled muscle and causes local tenderness. A second-degree muscle tear brings on sudden pain and swelling. This results in a loss of muscle strength. A third-degree tear is also called a rupture and must be surgically repaired. Most people do not consider a pulled muscle a threatening injury. True, it's not likely to make you miss many workouts, but you need to consider the consequences. First-degree injuries can become second-degree injuries. If you keep pushing through the pain of a first-degree muscle tear during your workouts, you risk developing a second-degree muscle tear.

C ontinual overuse of an already injured muscle can lead to more severe degrees of injury. A muscle is stretched when you hold it at the endpoint of its range of motion. Forcing a muscle beyond its range of motion causes muscle tears.

A frequently injured muscle group is the hamstrings. This occurs due to a lack of flexibility. When you move the muscle past its range of motion, overstretching of the muscle fibers results. The overstretching of the muscle fibers produces the muscle tear. This can occur when the opposing muscle group (also called the antagonist muscle group), in this case the quadricep muscle group, produces enough force to move the hamstrings past their range of motion. Treatment consists of the RICE method and possibly anti-inflammatory medication. Muscle injuries heal faster than other injuries because of the higher blood flow that muscles receive compared to tendons, bones, and ligaments. You can prevent many muscle injuries by practicing flexibility training regularly and properly warming up before strenuous or high-intensity workouts. Flexibility training improves the stretch of the muscles. A proper warm-up creates a muscle that is warm, and a warm muscle will stretch further.

A second-degree muscle tear requires you to stop exercising. Beyond this, treatment is the same as for a first-degree tear, with the addition of heat after 3 days of ice treatment. A third-degree muscle tear requires surgical repair and does not commonly occur in endurance athletes.

Injury to a Tendon

A tendon attaches muscle to bone. A relatively large muscle mass is connected to a relatively small area of bone by a relatively small amount of fibrous tissue (the tendon). This means the tendon is called upon to bear considerable stress. Tendons become strained when injured. Inflammation of a tendon is called tendinitis. Tendon injuries generally require more time to heal than injuries to muscles, because they receive less blood flow. General treatment is the RICE method. You can prevent many tendon injuries by practicing regular flexibility training and properly warming up before strenuous or high-intensity workouts. This is the same as methods to prevent muscle injuries because the tendon is actually a continuation of the muscle.

Injury to a Bone

There are different degrees of bone injuries. Bones can have microfractures (for example, shin splints), stress fractures, or compound fractures (the classic example of a broken bone). Compound fractures are not common among endurance athletes, but stress fractures are. Because bones receive a smaller percentage of blood flow than the muscles, bone injuries can seem relatively slow to heal. Microfractures tend to occur in areas of tendon attachment because of the tremendous force that is applied by the muscle during exercise. This force is transferred to the bone via the tendon, and it is at the point of attachment that the tendon can begin to pull away from the bone.

Stress fractures can develop anywhere a bone is subjected to a repeated force. Endurance athletes most often suffer them in the foot. Increasing the volume of training gradually is the best way to prevent stress fractures. The first line of treatment for a stress fracture is rest, but you can resume exercising if you feel little pain during activity.

A compound fracture can result from something traumatic like a bicycle crash. Professional medical treatment is mandatory.

Injury to a Ligament

Ligaments connect bone to bone. Injury to a ligament is called a *sprain*. Ligament injuries are slower to heal than muscle injuries, because ligaments receive less relative blood flow. The areas of your body where ligaments are most likely to be injured are the ankles and the knees. Most injuries to ligaments are acute (from a single occurrence) rather than chronic. An example of a ligament injury is twisting your ankle in a pothole. The first line of treatment is the RICE method.

Injury to a Nerve

Nerve injuries are not common in endurance sports, but they do occur. One example is subluxation (partial dislocation) of a vertebra, which puts pressure on a spinal nerve. Another is Morton's neuroma, which is a thickening of the nerve between the metatarsals (the bones in the front of the foot). Pain is signaled to the brain via nerve pathways. Stimulation of certain nerve endings tells you when any area of your body is experiencing pain. What feels like pain in your hip can result from a nerve in your spine being pressured due to poor alignment. Morton's neuroma can make your foot feel cramped, numb, or even like it's burning. You may think this pain is related to muscles, tendons, or even bones. Because nerve injury is unusual in endurance athletes and is likely to be the result of a biomechanical problem, seek out a professional for treatment.

Injury to the Skin

Skin injuries occur predominantly from friction. Typical skin injuries include blisters, heat rash, and road rash.

Most blisters occur on the feet and can usually be prevented by wearing properly fitted shoes and socks. You can use petroleum jelly to help reduce friction because it lubricates the rubbing surfaces.

Road rash is mild abrasions incurred when you fall off your bike and your skin scrapes against the pavement. It is generally not a cause for concern. However, once the skin has been broken, you must guard against infection. Wash the injury site and apply an antibiotic ointment.

Common Injuries

The most common injuries among multisport athletes are listed next. This is not a comprehensive list but is intended to help you recognize when an injury may be serious.

Foot Pain

The bottom of the foot is made up of a tendon sheath called the plantar (foot) fascia (band). Figure 10.1 gives a rough idea of what these tendons look like. Inflammation of this band is most noticeable when you wake up in the morning. You feel the pain close to the heel and toward the inside of the foot.

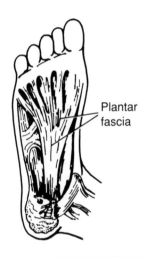

Plantar fascia

Figure 10.1   The plantar fascia forms a wide tendon sheath extending from the heel into the toes.

Pain in this area is called plantar fasciitis. Plantar fasciitis is probably caused by increasing the duration of exercise too quickly or wearing shoes that don't fit properly or don't provide adequate support. The RICE method is the first line of treatment used, although you may need to visit a professional medical person. The longer you've had the pain, the more likely it is that you need professional help.

Shin Splints

The term shin splints encompasses many lower leg pains (see Figure 10.2). In the truest sense, shin splints result when the muscles of the lower leg begin to pull off the inside of the lower leg bone (tibia). You can develop anterior and posterior shin splints, each caused by an imbalanced or overfatigued muscle group.

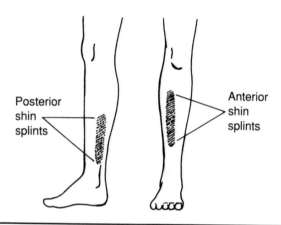

Figure 10.2   The shaded areas indicate the most common locations for shin splints.

You can best prevent shin splints by wearing proper footwear, gradually increasing your training volume, and practicing strength training. Treatment generally follows the RICE method, although you can relieve anterior shin splints somewhat by taping.

Runner's Knee

The injury commonly called runner's knee is known scientifically as chondromalacia patella. It is common among endurance athletes. Prolonged flexion (sitting too long) can cause chondromalacia patella, but it develops in endurance athletes for other reasons.

The first circumstance that causes chondromalacia patella in athletes is weak quadricep (thigh) muscles. The quadriceps keep the patella in the femoral groove. Weak quadriceps allow the patella to move out of the femoral groove. Once this occurs, the underside of the patella rubs against the femur (thighbone). Strength training is the proper follow-up after initial treatment—the RICE method and possibly anti-inflammatory medication. Do not continue the activity (most likely running) if you continue to experience pain.

The second condition that causes chondromalacia patella is overpronation. You'll remember from chapter 2 that pronation is the inward movement or rotation of your foot as it strikes the ground, when your ankle appears to bow slightly inward during contact. It occurs when the arch of your foot flattens as a result of bearing your weight. Pronation is normal and necessary. Without it your body would be unable to absorb much shock, and you'd be confined to running on ideal running surfaces. Overpronation, or hyperpronation, is an excessive rotation and can lead to greater stress on the ligaments, tendons, and muscles of the lower body. Underpronation, or lack of rotation, can lead to a number of foot injuries and possibly other lower body injuries.

The overpronating foot in turn results in an overrotated lower leg, which sends the patella sliding from side to side. After receiving the proper initial treatment (described previously), you must correct the poor biomechanics resulting from the overpronation. A podiatrist can help you with this, most likely by prescribing an orthotic device.

The third condition that causes chondromalacia patella in athletes is running repeatedly on the same side of a road that has too much roll or pitch. (Roads are pitched to allow for precipitation runoff.) The pitch causes the foot closer to the center of the road to overpronate. This is the easiest condition to correct, but you must initially treat it in the same manner as in the other two conditions.

Lateral Knee Pain

The iliotibial band is a continuation of the tensor fascia lata muscle that begins at your hip and continues down to just below your knee (see Figure 10.3). It is mostly connective tissue and plays an important role in stabilizing the knee.

The pain comes from an inflammation caused when the iliotibial band rubs over the outside of the knee. You may not feel the pain until after your workout, but the preceding activity is still what's responsible for the injury. This *iliotibial band friction syndrome* probably has structural causes, such as a tight iliotibial band; or biomechanical causes, such as running on a pitched surface, which results in one leg being overstretched. Proper treatment begins with the RICE method. Correcting your biomechanical errors should bring about rapid improvement. Correcting your structural problems requires practicing a regular flexibility program.

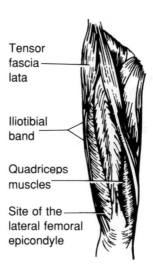

Tensor fascia lata

Iliotibial band

Quadriceps muscles

Site of the lateral femoral epicondyle

Figure 10.3 The iliotibial band extends along the outside of the thigh to just below the knee. Iliotibial band syndrome occurs at the outside of the knee.

Low Back Pain

In the workplace, more days of work are lost due to low back pain than to any other injury. To the endurance athlete, low back pain can result in many lost workouts. Low back pain is not one of the most common injuries among endurance athletes, but it's debilitating to those who suffer from it. Your back is made up of a combination of nerves, ligaments, bones, tendons, muscles, and disks (see Figure 10.4).

Back pain from running and biking commonly results for many reasons. If you experience low back pain, examine the following possibilities when seeking relief.

- A tight psoas muscle produces *lordosis* (an increased curvature of the lower back).
- A tight hamstring muscle makes proper knee flexion difficult, which can make it hard for you to rotate your pelvis forward. This makes bending forward on a bicycle problematic. A tight hamstring also hampers a full stride during running. This can place additional stress on your back.
- A serious nerve injury is *sciatica*, which requires medical attention. If you suffer from sciatica, numbness or pain can radiate down your entire leg.

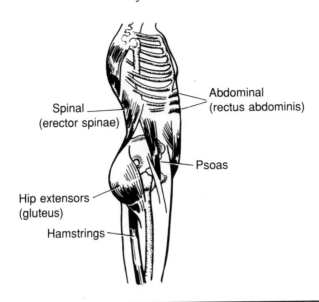

Figure 10.4 The muscle groups of the back and abdomen support the back and maintain posture.

- Remember from chapter 5 that running in the fatigued state results in more up-and-down movement of your center of gravity than when you're fresh. This additional vertical movement creates extra stress (from a greater vertical force being generated) that increases the impact of the other vertebrae on the spine.
- A knock-kneed runner has an exaggerated forward pelvic tilt. This also places additional stress on the lower back.
- Being overweight places an extra strain on your lower back. Ideally, only beginning endurance athletes have this problem. When your body fat drops, you'll find relief from many overuse injuries, and your performance should improve considerably as well.

Five muscle groups in the lower back (abdominal, psoas, spinal, hamstring, and gluteus) are responsible for supporting your body. Weakness in any of these muscle groups may be responsible for lower back pain. Strength training is useful in alleviating the pain, because stronger muscles can handle more stress. Flexibility training is most important in that many overuse injuries come from muscular imbalance (one muscle group is considerably shorter than either the opposing muscle group or the contralateral muscle group).

Shoulder Pain

Shoulder pain is commonly caused by *shoulder bursitis*. A bursa is a sac containing lubricating fluid, and when it is continually compressed from a movement like swimming, it can become inflamed.

The muscles that are directly responsible for the stability of the shoulder joint, and therefore the irritation of the bursa, are called the *rotator cuff* muscles. If you don't curtail or eliminate the movements that produce the bursitis, the injury becomes progressively worse. The tendons that connect the rotator cuff muscles to the bone can become inflamed; this condition is called tendinitis. If treatment does not begin at this point, the injury can eventually result in a rotator cuff tear (see Figure 10.5).

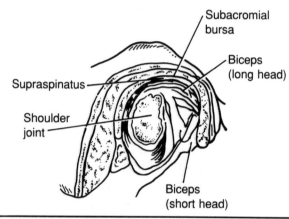

Figure 10.5 A side view of the shoulder, with the head toward the top of the illustration, revealing the multiple structures involved in shoulder bursitis and supraspinatus tendinitis.

The first line of treatment for shoulder pain is the RICE method, followed by anti-inflammatory medicine to reduce inflammation. Avoid exercises that require lifting your arm up and out to the side. It may be difficult to curtail this movement that is part of so many everyday activities, but keep in mind that any additional compression will aggravate the situation.

After every swim, get in the habit of stretching the muscles of the back of the arm (triceps), the shoulder (deltoids), the chest (pectorals), and the back (latissimus dorsi and trapezius). Doing this will help you reduce the likelihood of injury. Use Table 10.2 as an easy reference for treating your injuries.

Table 10.2
Injury Quick Reference Table

Location of pain	Pain seems worse when	First line of action	Possible causes
Foot	Rising from bed after sleep	RICE method	1. Rapid increase in training duration 2. Bad shoes
Shin	Beginning exercise	RICE method	Same as above
Kneecap	Exercising or sitting	RICE method	1. Weak quadriceps 2. Overpronation 3. Running on a pitched road
Outer knee	Exercising or just after	RICE method	1. Tight iliotibial band 2. Running on a pitched road 3. Cycling cleats improperly adjusted to allow knock-knees
Low back	Any time	RICE method	1. Tight psoas muscle 2. Tight hamstring muscle 3. Sciatica (nerve injury) 4. Knock-kneed running 5. Overweight
Shoulder	Exercising	RICE method	Poor swimming biomechanics

Part IV

Competing
and More

By now you surely must be eager to get out and apply what you've learned. Well, don't head out the door just yet. You need to put the finishing touches on your training to get ready for the race.

The week leading up to a triathlon is different from the rest of your training. In this section, we take you through that week. You'll learn how to ease off your regular schedule and how to eat for the big day.

Knowing what to do on race day will be easy after you learn a few important tips. From the morning of the race to the end of the day, we offer insight on what to expect, noting all the little details that might escape your attention (because of the excitement, of course).

We've also included some extra information that will interest many racers. Details on national organizations, race series, and additional readings complete this part.

Chapter 11

Race Week

During training, your muscles remain in a state of constant repair, and the body's carbohydrate stores are always in a semidepleted state. Both of these conditions are necessary if you want to increase your strength and endurance (the overload principle). When carbohydrate stores are constantly being depleted, they too adapt to take on greater reserves. Muscle enlargement (hypertrophy) and muscle strength develop most effectively when the body is in a semifatigued state. But because you can achieve optimal performance only when your body is fully recovered, as a triathlete you have to decide when training must diminish and full recovery—physical, mental, and nutritional—must take precedence. Therefore, in this chapter we'll first consider how you can enter into a state of optimal physical repair, and then how you can maximize your carbohydrate stores. This process is called the *training taper*.

The Final Workout

About 7 days before the day of competition, you'll need to enter into a state of physical and nutritional depletion; this represents the first stage of the training taper. Allowing more than a week can result in detraining, in which you may get out of shape. If you perform the depletion effort fewer than 5 days before the race, you might not fully recover in time for competition.

Consider the depletion workout as the grand finale of your training. What remains is minimal training and maximal eating. Probably the most effective depletion workout is to replicate as closely as possible the demands you will encounter on race day. Not only will you deplete the carbohydrate stores in the muscles you'll need for competition, but you'll also have the added confidence of knowing that you can go the distance.

Let's suppose that you want to taper for an international distance race, and the race is on a Sunday. On the Monday before the race, bike and run in the proper order as a combined workout and train close to the race distances. It is much more important to train at a high intensity than to cover a long distance, so don't dawdle. You should also do a swim workout, but this can take place either before or after the combined bike-and-run.

On Tuesday and Wednesday, go only about 40% of Sunday's distances, but maintain the same training pace. On Thursday and Friday, reduce the distances to 20% of Sunday's workout, yet keep the same pace. Saturday, limit yourself to a light, loose workout or even total rest.

The training taper just described may prove unrealistic if you are competing in long or ultra distance events. A very effective alternative is to deplete by exercising at high intensities in all three events. Figure 11.1 illustrates how much muscle glycogen you deplete while cycling at different intensities.

As you can see in Figure 11.1, although the exercise at 75% of maximum effort lasted the shortest time, the carbohydrate depletion was the most effective. Regardless of the technique you choose for depletion, you must reach a high level of fatigue by the time you complete your workout.

By fatiguing your body, you initiate carbohydrate depletion and begin the final muscle-rebuilding stage. As we mentioned previously, carbohydrate loading is a very specific process. Failing to adequately deplete all the carbohydrate stores in the muscles you'll use in competition will compromise your depletion effort. Skeletal muscle is the most important site for glycogen storage, but this fuel is not free to move from one muscle to another. It can be used only in the muscle in which it is stored. The

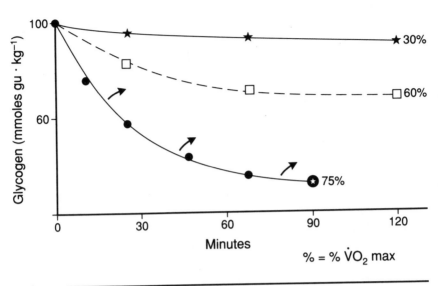

Figure 11.1 Rates of muscle glycogen depletion at different cycling intensities.

only general distribution center for carbohydrates is the liver, but its stores are very limited. Any muscle that is not adequately depleted and later supercompensated may call upon liver glycogen stores to provide energy for muscle contraction. This can eventually prove lethal; carbohydrates stored in the liver need to be reserved as fuel for nervous tissue function. How can you best bring about depletion? Simple. Deplete the swimming muscles by swimming, the cycling muscles by cycling, and the running muscles by running. That's all there is to it.

Carbohydrate Loading

The technique of carbo loading actually overfills all the carbohydrate stores in the body. Because the body's carbohydrate stores are somewhat limited, this technique becomes very attractive to those who are competing in races lasting longer than 1-1/2 hr. The basic principle behind carbo loading is rather peculiar. If you deprive the body of carbos when it wants them, the body will in turn store extra amounts when this precious fuel is finally made available. In a way you're playing a trick on your body, but it works!

Carbohydrate loading has undergone quite a metamorphosis since its introduction in the late 1960s. The initial technique began with a depletion phase that was a workout to exhaustion. Next, the athlete went 3 days with no carbos at all, followed by another exhaustive workout. For the next 3 days, the athlete ate all the carbohydrates in sight. Anyone who didn't get sick, psyched out, or injured following this procedure was sure to get diarrhea!

Fortunately, researchers have designed a much more reasonable program that yields about the same carbo-loading results as the initial technique. This approach is called the Sherman technique. Beginning 8 days before an important long-distance event, you attempt to exhaust your body's carbohydrate reserves using the muscles you'll need in competition. A triathlete should ideally perform near-exhaustive workouts in all three events. Remember, exercise should be at a high intensity rather than cover a long distance.

On the 2nd, 3rd, and 4th days, 50% of the calories you consume are in the form of carbohydrates, usually about 1,500 to 1,800 kcal worth. The rest of the diet is distributed equally between protein and fat. Exercise remains at the same intensity as in the exhaustive workouts done initially, but you cover only 40% of those distances.

During the final 3 days, you switch to a 70% carbohydrate diet, say, 2,000 to 2,400 kcal of carbohydrates. The remaining 30% of the calories are distributed equally between protein and fat. A typical meal series appears in Table 11.1.

Exercise remains at the same intensity, except now you reduce the distances to 20% of the original workout. The day before the race is a rest day, with your last meal being at least 18 hr before the starting time; otherwise your body won't have enough time to completely digest and process the meal. This technique is outlined in Figure 11.2.

Another alternative to carbo loading might be not loading any at all. Just by exercising and eating a high-carbohydrate diet on a regular basis, you'll almost double your muscle glycogen stores. Figure 11.3 compares these different techniques to levels found in a normal, nonactive muscle. In the final analysis, each triathlete must experiment with what works best for him or her. But if you try a carbo-loading technique, you'll gain weight. Every gram of carbohydrate is stored in 4 g of water. For some, this could amount to about a 5-lb water-weight gain, but you'll readily lose this during the race.

The Training Taper

Whether you plan to carbo load or not, you must taper off your workouts if you intend to compete at your best. When you are training properly,

Table 11.1
Typical Meal Series

Item	Quantity
Orange juice	1 cup
Cornflakes	3/4 cup
Banana	1 medium
Wheat toast	2 slices
Jelly	1 tablespoon
Skim milk	1 cup
560 calories; 84% carbohydrates	
Vegetable soup	1 cup
Chicken	2 ounces
White bread	2 slices
Applesauce	1 cup
Yogurt, low-fat	1 cup
627 calories; 71% carbohydrates	
Julienne salad made with:	
Lettuce	1 cup
Ham	1 ounce
Turkey	1 ounce
Pudding	1/2 cup
Grape juice	1 cup
560 calories; 82% carbohydrates	
Pork and beans	1 cup
Crackers	10
Carrot sticks	5 in. carrot
Fruit salad	1/2 cup
Skim milk	1 cup
677 calories; 66% carbohydrates	
Total calories for all meals: 2,424	
Total % carbohydrates for all meals: 71%	

the microstructure of your muscles remains in a state of constant microtearing and rebuilding. This constant tearing and repairing is normal, because the repair makes the muscle stronger than it was before the tear. In other words, skeletal muscle rebuilds to greater capacities than previous levels. When you lift weight, your muscles enlarge in response to the greater demands.

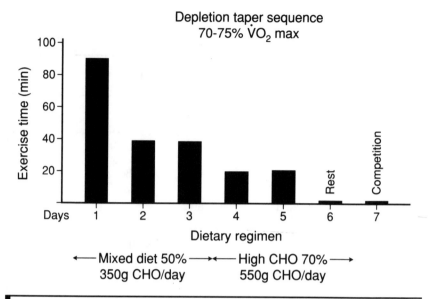

Figure 11.2 The Sherman technique of carbohydrate loading.

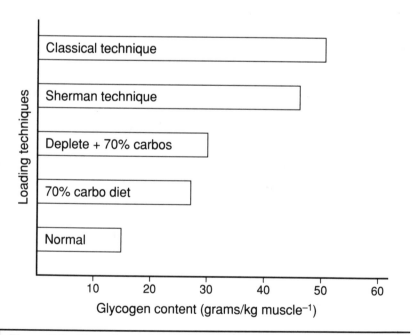

Figure 11.3 Comparisons of the various carbohydrate-loading techniques.

The way triathletes train will not enlarge their muscles, but it will make them more aerobic. Although these developments demonstrate the body's remarkable ability to adapt, there is risk involved when abused. Whenever the body is in a state of repair, the risk of injury to the muscles and connective tissues increases. Athletes who neglect to give the body adequate time and nutrition for the repair process to occur may eventually fall prey to injury and illness. Sooner or later, the body gets the rest it needs. Your main objective for the taper period should be full recovery.

A technique for proper recovery is called *active recovery*. The principle involved is that some activity needs to continue during the recovery period so that (a) optimal production of chemicals (enzymes) needed to process the energy nutrients continues; (b) you don't start to detrain, or lose conditioning; and (c) you don't end up with muscle and joint stiffness. Also, active recovery enhances the healing process discussed previously. As we mentioned, the best way to recover is not to decrease exercise intensity, but to cut back on distance.

The Carbo-Loading Party

The pregame meal, or carbo-loading party, is a social ritual that should have no place in sport. Theoretically, race participants gather the night before the big race to load up on carbohydrates. Instead, most of them end up loading fats. Sure, spaghetti contains some carbohydrates, but what about the meatballs and the sauce? What's the caloric distribution of a banana cream pie? Athletes who are uninformed and unfamiliar with proper food choices often load too much fat at these parties. The social pressure to make food taste good requires supplementing bland-tasting carbohydrates with plenty of fat. Prudent endurance athletes who consider performance more important than satiety will avoid fat- and protein-oriented pregame foods. A sample food plan for carbo-loading needs is provided in Table 11.2.

The second problem with the carbo-loading party is its timing. Eating a large meal the night before the race is unwise because the food residue will not clear the body in such a short period. Sponsors of the Hawaiian Ironman triathlon hold their carbo-loading party 2 nights before the race. Not only is this more nutritionally sound, but it also helps to keep participants' anxiety levels under control by spreading out prerace hype. Your last large meal should be no less than 24 hr before the race, preferably closer to 36 hr. After that point, eat only light carbohydrate meals, such

Table 11.2
Daily Food Plan for Carbohydrate Loading

Dietary sources of carbohydrate, protein, and fat	Amounts and calories	Grams of carbohydrate, protein, and fat
Meat, fish, poultry, eggs, cheese Select low-fat items	6–8 ounces Calories: 330–440	0 grams carbohydrate 42–56 grams protein 18–24 grams fat
Breads, cereals, and grain products	10–20 servings Calories: 800–1600	150–300 grams carbohydrate 24–60 grams protein
Vegetables, high calorie (such as corn)	4 servings Calories: 280	60 grams carbohydrate 8 grams protein
Fruits	4 servings Calories: 240	60 grams carbohydrate
Fats and oils	2–4 teaspoons Calories: 90–180	10–20 grams fat
Milk, skim	2 servings Calories: 180	24 grams carbohydrate 16 grams protein
Desserts, like pie	2 servings Calories: 700	102 grams carbohydrate 6 grams protein 30 grams fat
Beverages, naturally sweetened	8–24 ounces Calories: 80–240	20–60 grams carbohydrate
Water	8 or more servings Calories: 0	
Total calories	2700–3860	

Total grams and approximate % of dietary calories
Carbohydrate	416–606	65%
Protein	96–146	15%
Fat	58–74	20%

as oatmeal, toast without butter, orange juice, bananas and other fruit, or your favorite pasta-only dish.

Other Taper Week Concerns

During taper week, you'll probably find you have extra time on your hands. For some, cutting back training time to 40% provides an extra 3 or 4 hours in the day. Idleness can create anxiety, so you'll no doubt welcome the chance to finalize some triathlon-related matters. Two tasks you must deal with during taper week are bike maintenance and becoming familiar with the course.

Because you are not allowed help in repairing your equipment after the race starts, you must troubleshoot everything possible ahead of time. We recommend that you dismantle all parts with bearings, inspect them for pitting or excessive wear, regrease them, and then reassemble. Inspect all cables for fraying or rust. Go over spoke tension and wheel trueness thoroughly. Perform this work early enough in your taper week so that you can road check all adjustments at least twice.

Your next, and certainly the most crucial, step is to inspect and install your best tires. Most competitors have a set of tires they use strictly for racing. Before installing them, inspect the entire surface of the tire for any pieces of glass or rock embedded deep in the rubber. These specks can eventually break through the tire without warning.

Another prerace task is becoming familiar with the race course. We've heard competitors say they prefer not knowing the course ahead of time; this is foolish. Much of your race strategy depends on knowing the course, because the way you distribute your energy depends on what you'll encounter throughout the race. As you review the course, make sure that your bike is adequately geared for the hills and that you know the route. Local triathlons are notorious for assuming that each competitor knows the route and often neglect to provide course marshals at key intersections.

When you have prepared properly, confidence will replace doubt. Even though you'll naturally reflect on your past training, be sure to get plenty of sleep and try to relax and think about other things. Enjoy the taper week. To some it is the calm before the storm. For new triathletes, it is a week of excitement and anticipation.

Chapter 12

Race Day

The vast majority of this day's outcome has been predetermined. If you trained well, if you tapered and loaded carbohydrates correctly, and if you've cared for your equipment well, you'll almost certainly perform up to your expectations. Obviously, your performance will require a tremendous amount of hard work plus a healthy dose of luck along the way. In this chapter we will consider all phases of race day in the hope that you can optimize the controllable factors and be better prepared for the unexpected. As you gain racing experience you'll better understand the issues presented here and no doubt will gain your own valuable insights.

Personalized Race Strategy

Well before entering the water, you should have developed a race strategy based on your personal strengths and weaknesses. The unpredictable competition is one of the most interesting aspects of the triathlon. The first person out of the water, for instance, may end up in the back of the pack by the race's end. Most triathlons now publicize the best performances in each of the three events. Triathletes know this, and many treat the triathlon as a single event in hopes of being recognized in their strongest area, even though they'll never finish high in the overall standings. Therefore, don't be discouraged if someone zips by you; you may overtake that competitor later in the race. Remember, in the end, the tortoise beat the hare.

Because of the unique features of triathlons, we strongly suggest that you know and go your own pace. Those who get caught up in the surrounding competition risk running out of energy before the demands of the competition are met. This recommendation is founded upon the need to conserve energy. The very nature of the triathlon requires you to maintain a steady pace and to be patient.

Fluid and Fuel Replacement

Before the actual race, you need to develop a strategy for dealing with the two biggest physiological problems associated with endurance competition: dehydration and depletion of fuel reserves. In chapter 8 we discussed the contradictory nature of these two problems. Whenever you consume sugar-based liquids, you experience a delay in getting fluids out of the stomach. Consequently, when your need for water replacement is critical (as in high temperatures and humid conditions), you can use water or sport drinks with dilute quantities of sugar.

The decision as to how concentrated a drink can be before your body cannot tolerate it well will come as a result of trial and error. For this reason, you must experiment with energy-replacement drinks during your *training* days. If the day is cool and dehydration poses little threat, you can consume sugar-based drinks to add some energy to tired muscles. Try the commercial drinks at the suggested concentrations. Experiment with diluting them or adding more powder.

Another important consideration is when to begin replacing the water and energy you use in exercise. If it is a hot or humid day begin replacing water well in advance of when you feel thirsty. You need to practice a technique called hyperhydration. About 30 min before the start of your race or training session, consume 8 to 16 oz of water, even though you may not be thirsty. This technique will significantly delay dehydration. Practice this technique ahead of time so you learn how much water your stomach will tolerate. Make sure you don't drink too far in advance of the start of your workout; otherwise your body will convert this much-needed water into urine.

During the race or workout, drink frequently and regularly. The stomach can process about 8-1/2 oz of fluid every 10 or 15 min, and cold drinks seem to work best. On the bike, you should go through about two standard-size water bottles every hour. The bike phase is by far the best time to consume sugar-based drinks. If you wait until the run phase, you won't have enough time to process the sugar into usable energy. Converting sugar into energy generally takes about 30 min at rest, but much longer during exercise because blood flow to the stomach is reduced significantly. Remember, when in doubt, drink water!

Racing Attire

More and more races allow the use of wet suits in cold water. Current regulations are provided in chapter 2, but regulations are subject to change, so consult your race director for the race rules. When racing conditions do allow participants to use wet suits, wear one if at all possible. They hold in valuable body heat and add significant buoyancy, enabling you to float on the surface of the water. Overall, you'll swim more efficiently and conserve valuable energy.

Race officials often require participants to wear swim caps, as these aid in rescue attempts. Caps also reduce the drag created by loose hair and can prevent heat loss through the head in cold water. When the water is below 78 °F or so, consider wearing two or three caps. Goggles are essential in salt water and in chlorinated water but can sometimes be omitted in shorter, freshwater swims. Goggles can leak, fog up, and become uncomfortable, so if you intend to use them in your race, wear them in practice so you can make all necessary adjustments in advance of competition. If you choose not to wear goggles, you risk scratching a cornea or incurring other eye injuries while swimming in crowded conditions.

What you wear for the rest of the race depends on several factors. Most competitors never change out of their swimsuits in shorter triathlons. They simply pull cycling shorts and running shorts over them. In effect, they use swimsuits as underwear. This practice saves valuable time in the transitions. If you intend to cycle or run in just your swimsuit, practice this well in advance of the race. You might experience a lot of chafing as well as miss the padding of cycling shorts.

In longer races, most triathletes prefer wearing traditional cycling and running wear. Why? Long rides inevitably cause saddle soreness. When this happens, you may find yourself moving around on the saddle, standing up while riding, and so on. Well-padded riding shorts will aid greatly in delaying this discomfort.

Another decision you must make before race time is whether to wear cycling shoes. Cycling shoes can definitely improve your pedaling technique, creating greater efficiency on the bike.

In shorter races, though, the time you save by wearing cycling shoes may not compensate for the time you lose when changing from cycling to running shoes. If you have a clipless pedal system on your bike, the decision is made for you: You will wear cycling shoes. If you have a standard pedal system, you can wear running shoes while cycling. Cycling shoes are stiff with hard soles. They lock into the pedal so they cannot slip off during the pedal stroke. By contrast, running shoes are soft, wide at the sole, and very flexible. Some of the energy you apply to the pedals will be absorbed in the shoe. In addition, you cannot apply proper pedal technique when cycling in running shoes. Even if the cycling course is short, you still might decide to wear cycling shoes if, for instance, the course is hilly or you have knee problems.

Finally, choose the color of your sports clothing with regard to typical race-day temperatures. If the day is expected to be hot, light-colored cotton or nylon clothing will offer the greatest cooling. If the day is expected to be cold, layered, dark-colored clothing is the better choice. As the temperature rises or as you heat up, you can peel off the layers as appropriate and wrap them around your waist.

Changing weather conditions often catch competitors off guard and can create havoc with your prerace plans. Many competitors use rain, tremendous head winds, or blazing heat as excuses for poor performances. Remember these same conditions affect all competitors; you must simply alter your race plans accordingly. If you can keep your spirits high during these times, inclement weather will almost always work to your advantage. Poor weather may slow your finish time, but don't be surprised to find that you finish higher than you expected.

The Big Day

Your race day breakfast should more or less "top off" the carbohydrate reserves that you might have spent since your last meal. One possibility consists of orange juice, toast and jelly without butter, and oatmeal with brown sugar. Eat about 2 to 3 hr before the start of your race.

Arrive at the race site at least 1 hr before the start. Once at the race site, check in and have your race number marked on your body. You must also place race numbers on your running and cycling clothing as well as on your bike. Most races stagger the start based on age, sex, ability, or all three. Check to see when your race group is scheduled to begin so you can determine when to begin warming up and hyperhydrating. In bigger races, some competitors will still be waiting for their swim start when the elite racers are already returning from their bike rides, so warming up at the right time requires careful attention.

Whether you include cycling and running as part of your warm-up ritual is a matter of personal choice. But a proper swim warm-up is essential, and it must be the last thing you do before the race. Your swim preparation should begin about 30 min before and end about 10 min before the start of your race. This way you can have full recovery, but blood flow remains in the exercising muscles. In general, do a full range of motion exercises slowly. Work the neck, shoulder, wrist, and ankles.

Racing Tips

Even in the most organized and well-supervised races, certain problems are bound to occur. These surprises can be frustrating and even traumatic. Your ability to react properly may well spare you from race withdrawal! Realize first that triathlon training cannot prepare you for a number of distractions you'll encounter only when racing. For instance, how do you train for the possibility of having your goggles kicked loose, or someone swimming into your stroke? The seasoned triathlete realizes that problems like these happen to everyone, and no one is purposely singling you out. Experienced triathletes are able to adjust to these inconveniences and continue competing without being affected emotionally. The purpose of this section is to investigate potential problem areas to help you avoid some of the race trauma associated with triathlons.

Swim Phase

Swim starts vary with each triathlon, but most races stagger start the swim phase. Starting times generally are by age, with the youngest competitors going first, but in some races ability enters the formula as well. Professional-class triathletes may go first in large races. In the Ironman, on the other hand, everyone begins at 7 a.m. This type of mass start offers both competitors and spectators the benefit of viewing the competition. The first person to finish is the absolute winner.

In mass starts and large races with staggered starting times, you must self-seed. This means that the best swimmers move to the front and the poorest swimmers to the back. Please go along with this advice, even if it costs you a few seconds in your overall finish time. Slow swimmers who start ahead of faster ones stand an excellent chance of having competitors actually swim right up their backs. Local triathlons usually attract a less intense group of competitors, and crowded conditions and the related problems seldom occur. Consider entering some local triathlons of this type before attempting larger races with more difficult, crowded starts.

As you begin the swim, concentrate on going straight and maintaining proper stroke technique. Inevitably, other competitors will interrupt your kick and your arm stroke. But realize that they too are struggling for available water space and are not intentionally breaking up your stroke.

On the positive side of the swim phase, look for opportunities to draft off other swimmers. This technique is similar to bicycle drafting and can reduce your work output by as much as 30%. Also, if you find yourself getting fatigued, switch temporarily to an alternate stroke, but only as a last resort. The stroke with which you have trained will always be the most efficient, and you should use it as long as possible.

Your main concern in open-water swimming is going straight. A 1.5-km swim can easily become a 2-km swim if you have not mastered this. As discussed in chapter 3, swimming straight involves sighting both forward and to the side. Your success in the swim phase depends on whether you've trained adequately in open water and practiced the techniques of front and side sighting.

Swim-to-Bike Transition

From a physical point of view, the swim-to-bike transition is by far the easier one in the triathlon. The upper body, fatigued from the swim, can now rest while the legs assume exercise responsibilities. But you may have to run a fair distance between the water and your bike. It sounds hard to believe, but some triathletes have run close to a mile during this transition. For this reason, pay close attention to where your bike is.

The clothing you change into is a matter of personal preference, but many competitors preparing to ride an hour or less prefer to either keep their swimsuits on or slip riding shorts over them. On longer races, it might be worth changing out of your swimsuit if changing quarters are available. When riding long distances, comfort is critical, and swimsuits provide no benefit. Some competitors keep a bedpan full of water in their changing areas for rinsing sand from their feet before they put on their shoes.

Bike Phase

A wise triathlete will begin the bike phase using a moderate pedal cadence with minimal resistance. This technique is important because it reroutes blood from the swimming muscles to the cycling muscles.

If your race is expected to draw a large crowd, watch for pedestrians, children, and even dogs crossing the street into your path. In one Ironman race a competitor hit someone crossing the street, fell from the bike and was knocked unconscious, and was eliminated from the competition. Be prepared for these types of problems whenever crowds are gathered. Once you've passed the spectators, settle into a comfortable riding position; the cycling phase in the triathlon is often quite long. Before you get too comfortable, however, realize that there's another crowd you need to confront throughout the remainder of the race—slower cyclists. They can swing into your path quite abruptly and even cause a crash. In competition, you need to continually focus your eyes on the bicycle traffic ahead.

Other congested areas that require your attention are aid stations. Make sure that you are clear of other cyclists when you approach them. When you want food or drink, forewarn, and even point to your intended exchange person. Cyclists will weave in and out unpredictably, so beware.

Also of concern to you are flat tires and mechanical failures. The effect of a flat tire is probably more psychological than it is detrimental to your overall race progress, because a well-trained, well-equipped cyclist can change a tire in 2 min. Tubular tires (sew-ups) can be changed very quickly, and you can also use a compressed air cartridge to fill it up. But while you're making the repair, competitors speed by you, and you may feel your desire to remain competitive dwindle.

Mechanical failures other than flats seldom occur if you've kept your bike well maintained and adjusted. But because you must make all your own repairs, we suggest carrying along flat-repair equipment, a spoke wrench, and allen wrenches. You'll need the spoke wrench if you pop a spoke. After you remove the broken spoke, use the spoke wrench to loosen the spokes on both sides of the broken one to bring the wheel true enough so it doesn't rub on the brake pads. You can replace the spoke and retrue the wheel after the race. Allen wrenches are used to adjust and tighten just about every bolt on bikes now, so you need a set of three or four for all adjustments.

The chain can fall off the front chain rings, but with practice, you should be able to properly replace the chain without even getting off your bike. If it falls off the inside (small) chain ring, reach down and start the chain back on from the underside and pedal backward. If the chain falls off on the outside or large chain ring, continue pedaling slowly while moving your front derailleur to the inside. If the chain doesn't catch on the crank arm, it will go right on without your even touching it.

On longer bike phases such as in an ultra distance triathlon, inevitably you will get sore while riding, especially in the buttocks, back, neck, and hands. The degree of soreness you'll experience is directly related to the success of your bike training program. But even highly trained cyclists get sore, so change your position a few times during your ride. Consider out-of-saddle climbing when confronting some of the uphills to temporarily relieve soreness. In tailwinds and on downhills, accelerate to high speeds and then coast in a tucked position. Not only does this rest help relieve soreness, but it is efficient as well.

Finally, when you approach the finish of the bike phase, focus your thoughts on running instead of showing off with a strong bike finish. Run preparation actually begins on the bike as you reduce your pedal effort to create a smoother, less intense cycling spin. When you finally dismount, your legs may act unpredictably, so be careful not to slip or fall while walking on your cycling shoes.

Bike-to-Run Transition

This transition is the most dangerous time of the race. Cyclists are sprinting to the finish area, runners are emerging onto the running course, officials are checking numbers and finish times, and spectators are lining the course. In United States Triathlon Series (USTS) races, competitors are still finishing the swim phase while all these other activities are going on.

This transition, unlike the previous one, presents some real challenges physically. After you've held your body in the riding position for such a long time, the more upright posture you need in running comes as a welcome relief, but you must execute it gingerly. Expect your leg muscles to have difficulty supporting your body weight. Realize also that your legs are sending blood mainly to the cycling muscles and not to the running muscles. Taking off as if you've properly warmed up for running will expose you to a risk of muscle and tendon injury and load your running muscles with lactic acid. So be prepared to run as if you have no knees, and begin at a slow pace until your blood is rerouted into the muscles that need it.

The Run Phase

During this phase of the race, you have the greatest chance to succeed or fail depending on your level of conditioning and on how well you survived the bike phase. Success is almost assured if you have effectively trained by the fatigued-run training technique outlined in chapter 5. If properly trained, your body will be accustomed to the unusual running form, to a slower pace, and to supporting your total weight. People who train inadequately for the run phase risk premature carbohydrate depletion and premature exhaustion. Assuming you are well trained for this phase of the triathlon, let's consider the problem areas you might encounter during the run.

Probably your biggest concern in the run phase is dehydration. People tend to be so afraid of stomach cramps resulting from fluids bouncing around in the stomach that they dehydrate. Make sure you drink at every aid station, and try to drink plenty. We suggest getting a full cup of ice water at each station, drinking about half of it, and then folding the top of the cup to seal off the rest of the water. Carry this cup like a lunch bucket and take occasional sips until the cup is empty. This system allows you to drink nearly continuously without needing to take large gulps.

If sponges are offered at the aid stations, use them carefully to prevent the legs from getting wet. If water runs down your leg, it ends up in your shoes, causing blisters. Don't consume food during the run phase. It can cause side aches and generally will not get digested in time to offer the body any usable energy during the race.

Knowing how much energy you have in reserve for the run phase is impossible to estimate, so make every effort to run efficiently. If you find yourself running out of carbohydrates, quickly consume some simple sugar such as a few orange sections, soda pop, or a sport drink, and temporarily decrease your pace until the symptoms subside. Stick to your training pace, don't get caught up in the competition, and make your final sprint only when the finish line is in sight.

If you set realistic goals, train effectively, and know and go your own pace, triathlon racing can be the ultimate reward for all your training. Unforeseen problems will occur; they occur for all competitors. The weather, fellow competitors, equipment, and your race strategy can all become problems. View your problems as challenges. Dealing with these challenges successfully is the mark of a true competitor. Good luck, and remember, the more effectively you train, the luckier you'll be!

Chapter 13

More Than Competition

You have completed a tremendous amount of material. If you apply what you've learned in the previous chapters, you are ready to race triathlons! This chapter provides you with background or more detailed information on all three components of the triathlon.

National Organizations

To completely immerse yourself in the triathlon scene and to be licensed to race in sanctioned races, you should join the Triathlon Federation

USA. Membership includes a license, valuable insurance, a publication (*Triathlon Times*), the ability to be ranked nationally after competing in any sanctioned race, and numerous discounts on airline flights and merchandise for an annual membership fee of $25. For more information call or write

Triathlon Federation USA
P.O. Box 15820
Colorado Springs, CO 80935-5820
(719) 597-9090

The following organizations specialize in one of the three sports that comprise the triathlon. If you have specific questions about a sport, call the appropriate organization.

United States Swimming
1750 E. Boulder St.
Colorado Springs, CO 80909
(719) 578-4578
The annual membership fee is $20, plus
local fees of about $5.

United States Cycling Federation
1750 E. Boulder St.
Colorado Springs, CO 80909
(719) 578-4581
The annual membership fee is $32.

USA Track and Field
P.O. Box 120
Indianapolis, IN 46206
(317) 261-0500
The annual membership fee is $12.

Other Organizations

Ironman Mainland Office World Triathlon Corporation
1570 U.S. Highway 19N
Tarpon Springs, FL 34689
(813) 943-4767 (phone)
(813) 938-3328 (fax)

League of American Wheelmen (LAW)
6707 Whitestone Rd., Suite 209
Baltimore, MD 21207
(301) 944-3399

Road Runners Clubs of America (RRCA)
629 S. Washington St.
Alexandria, VA 22314
(703) 836-0558

TRI-CANADA
1154 W. 24th St.
N. Vancouver, BC V6V2J2
(604) 987-0092

ULTRA Marathon Cycling Association
4790 Irvine Blvd., #105-111
Irvine, CA 92720
(714) 544-1701

United States Master Swimming
2 Peter Ave.
Rutland, MA 01543
(508) 886-6631

Important Race Series

The race series that draws the most participants is the Bud Light Triathlon Series. These are international distance races (1.5-km swim, 40-km bike, 10-km run) and sprint distance races (0.75-km swim, 20-km bike, 5-km run).

For more information write
CAT Sports, Inc.
5962 La Place Ct. #145
Carlsbad, CA 92008
(619) 221-5555

For those of you who still are not convinced that swimming is right for you, or if you want a race to prepare you for a coming triathlon, try a duathlon. The distances are 5-km run, 30-km bike, and 5-km run. In 1992 the Coors Light Duathlon Series was tremendously popular. However, Coors will no longer be sponsoring the race series.

For more information write

Hamilton Events
2680 Surrey Lane
West Linn, OR 97068
(503) 655-4687, (503) 655-4392 (fax)

A great race series for women only is the Danskin Women's Triathlon
Series. The race distances are as follows: 0.75-km swim, 20-km bike, and
5-km run. These distances make the Danskin an outstanding race for
beginners. But elite females love the series as well, and they finish the
race in less than an hour.
For more information write

Lynn Colangelo
Danskin
111 W. 40th, 18th Floor
New York, NY 10018
(800) 452-9526

The Ironman Triathlon World Championship Series might be only a
dream for most of us, but it is worth mentioning:

World Triathlon Corporation
1570 U.S. Highway 19N
Tarpon Springs, FL 34689
(813) 943-4767 (phone)
(813) 938-3328 (fax)

Periodicals

Bicycle Guide
P.O. Box 55729
Boulder, CO 80322
(800) 456-6501

Bicycling
33 E. Minor St.
Emmaus, PA 18098
(800) 441-7761

Competitor
2120 Jimmy Durante Blvd., Suite R
Del Mar, CA 92014
(619) 793-2711

Cycling Science
P.O. Box 1510
Mount Shasta, CA 96067
(916) 938-4411

Runner's World
33 E. Minor St.
Emmaus, PA 18098
(800) 441-7761

Running Times
P.O. Box 16927
North Hollywood, CA 91615
(213) 858-7100

Triathlete
1415 Third St., Suite 303
Santa Monica, CA 90401
(800) 441-1666

Triathlon Today
P.O. Box 1587
Ann Arbor, MI 48106
(800) 346-5902

Velonews
P.O. Box 55729
Boulder, CO 80322
(800) 825-0061

Winning
1127 Hamilton St.
Allentown, PA 18101
(800) 441-1666

Books

Biathlon Training and Racing, Kenny Souza, Contemporary Books, 1989.

Bicycle Road Racing, Eddie Borysewicz, Vitesse Press, 1985.

The Complete Triathlon Distance Training Manual, Bob Johnson and Patricia Braggs, Health Science, 1982.

Dave Scott's Triathlon Training, Dave Scott, Simon and Schuster, 1986.

The Fit Swimmer: 120 Workouts and Training Tips, Marianne Brems, Contemporary Books, 1984.

Greg LeMond's Complete Book of Cycling, Greg LeMond, Putnam Publishing Group, 1988.

The High Performance Triathlete, Katherine Vaz and Barcley Krus, Contemporary Books, 1985.

Iron Will, Mike Plant, Contemporary Books, 1987.

Mark Allen's Total Triathlete, Mark Allen, Contemporary Books, 1988.

Science of Cycling, Ed Burke, Human Kinetics, 1986.

Science of Triathlon Training and Competition, Glenn Town, Human Kinetics, 1985.

Scott Tinley's Winning Triathlon, Scott Tinley, Contemporary Books, 1986.

Serious Training for Serious Athletes, Rob Sleamaker, Human Kinetics, 1989.

Stretching, Bob Anderson, Shelter Publications, 1980.

Training and Racing Biathlons, Mark Sisson, Primal Urge Press, 1989.

Triathlon—A Triple Fitness Sport, Sally Edwards, Contemporary Books, 1985.

Triathlon—Going the Distance, Mike Plant, Contemporary Books, 1987.

Triathloning for Ordinary Mortals, Dr. Steven Jonas, Norton, 1986.

Triathlon Training and Racing Book, Sally Edwards, Contemporary Books, 1985.

The Two Wheeled Athlete, Ed Burke, Vitesse Press, 1986.

Index

race day tips for, 202, 204
training for, 92, 98, 129
Travel, time required for, 9
Triathlon bicycles, 20-22. *See also* Bicycles
Triathlons
bibliography on, 211-212
distances for, 4, 5-6
Half-Ironman triathlon, 6
history of, 3-4
international distance, 5, 103-104, 142, 143
Ironman triathlon, 3-4, 6, 78, 201, 203, 210
long distance, 6, 141, 143
organizations, 207-209
race day tips for, 197-205
race information sources, 209-210
sprint distance, 5, 142, 143
ultra distance, 6, 141, 143
United States Triathlon Series (USTS), 204

U

Ultra distance triathlons, 6, 141, 143
Underpronation, 179
United States Cycling Federation (USCF), 31
United States Triathlon Series (USTS), 204

V

Vessel shaping (swimming body position), 55-57, 63, 67, 69
Virgin, Craig, 86
Vitamins, 153-154, 155-156

Volume (time required) for training. *See also* Duration for training
in general, 5, 7, 8, 9-10
and injury prevention, 178
in year-round systematic training, 117-118, 128, 131

W

Warm-ups/cool-downs
in general, 111-112
for lactic-anaerobic training, 105
for races, 201
for strength training, 108, 123, 134
Water. *See* Dehydration, prevention of
Water bottles, 31
Weather, during races, 200
Weight control, 8
Wet suits, 13-14, 66-67, 199
Wheels, 24-29
Wind resistance. *See* Aerodynamics of bicycling

Y

Year-round systematic training
base stage of, 117, 119-128
intensity stage of, 117, 119, 120, 121, 128-131
overview of, 117, 118-119
peak stage of, 117, 119, 120, 121, 131-135
race stage of, 119, 120, 121, 135-137
recovery stage of, 119, 120, 121, 128, 137-139
sample schedules for, 125-128, 130, 132-133, 134, 136, 138-139
volume for, 117-118, 128, 131

About the Authors

Glenn Town   **Todd Kearney**

Swim, Bike, Run co-author Glenn Town is a triathlete who knows the rigors of training and competition; he was the 24th-place finisher in the 1983 Ironman World Triathlon Championship. He also directs the exercise physiology laboratory at Wheaton College in Wheaton, Illinois, where he is also a professor of exercise physiology. He is a fellow in the American College of Sports Medicine (ACSM) and science editor for *Triathlete* magazine. Dr. Town is the author of *Science of Triathlon Training and Competition*.

Todd Kearney also has both the professional's and the participant's views of the triathlon. As an exercise trainer, he has worked with endurance athletes since 1982; as an athlete, he has participated in many endurance events, including the Ironman distance ESPRIT triathlon and other half Ironman triathlons. He is a member of the ACSM and Triathlon Federation/USA and the author of several articles on triathlon training, including "Realistic Training for Triathletes," published in *Triathlete* magazine.